WHAT IS THE BOOK OF 1 SAMUEL?

Kids' Guides to God's Word Series

What Is the Book of Genesis?
What Is the Book of Exodus?
What Is the Book of Leviticus?
What Is the Book of Numbers?
What Is the Book of Deuteronomy?
What Is the Book of Joshua?
What Is the Book of Judges?
What Is the Book of Ruth?
What Is the Book of 1 Samuel?
What Is the Book of 2 Samuel?
What Is the Book of 1 Kings?
What Is the Book of 2 Kings?
What Are the Books of 1–2 Chronicles?
What Are the Books of Ezra & Nehemiah?
What Is the Book of Esther?
What Is the Book of Job?
What Is the Book of Psalms?
What Is the Book of Proverbs?
What Is the Book of Ecclesiastes?
What Are the Books of Song of Songs &
Lamentations?
What Is the Book of Isaiah?
What Is the Book of Jeremiah?
What Is the Book of Ezekiel?
What Is the Book of Daniel?
What Are the Books of Hosea–Micah?
What Are the Books of Nahum–Malachi?

What Is the Gospel of Matthew?
What Is the Gospel of Mark?
What Is the Gospel of Luke?
What Is the Gospel of John?
What Is the Book of Acts?
What Is the Book of Romans?
What Is the Book of 1 Corinthians?
What Is the Book of 2 Corinthians?
What Is the Book of Galatians?
What Is the Book of Ephesians?
What Is the Book of Philippians?
What Are the Books of Colossians
& Philemon?
What Are the Books of 1–2 Thessalonians?
What Are the Books of 1–2 Timothy & Titus?
What Is the Book of Hebrews?
What Is the Book of James?
What Are the Books of 1–2 Peter & Jude?
What Are the Books of 1-3 John?
What Is the Book of Revelation?

What Is the Book of
1 SAMUEL?

Michael Whitworth

ISBN 978-1-971767-07-9

Published by Start2Finish
Bend, Oregon 97702
start2finish.org

Printed in the United States of America
30 29 28 27 26   1 2 3 4 5

CONTENTS

INTRODUCTION

Have you ever watched a championship game where everything was on the line? The crowd is roaring. The clock is ticking down. One team has been dominant for years, but now they're struggling. Their star player is injured, their coach is making bad calls, and you can feel the momentum shifting. Meanwhile, there's this rookie on the other team—someone nobody expected much from—who keeps making impossible plays. Every time he touches the ball, something amazing happens.

You know how this ends. The old champion falls. The new king rises. But what makes it compelling isn't just the final score—it's watching it unfold, seeing the turning point, and understanding *why* the change had to happen.

That's the book of 1 Samuel. It's the story of Israel's greatest transition—from the wild chaos of the judges to the establishment of the monarchy. It's the story of how one kingdom ended and another began. And at its heart, it's about two men who couldn't be more different: Saul, the king who had everything and lost it all, and David, the shepherd boy who had nothing and gained a throne.

But it's also about something deeper. It's about what God looks for in the people he chooses to use. It's about the difference between outward appearance and the condition of the heart. It's about what happens when we demand our own way instead of trusting God's plan.

And it's about a question that echoes through the whole book and into our own lives: What kind of person does God want me to be?

WHERE WE'VE BEEN

If you've been following the story of Israel through the Old Testament, you know things have been rough. After Joshua led the people into the Promised Land, they were supposed to drive out the remaining Canaanites and stay faithful to God. They didn't. The book of Judges tells the ugly story of what happened next—cycles of sin, oppression, and rescue that spiraled downward for three hundred years. "Everyone did what was right in his own eyes," the book keeps telling us, and what seemed right in their eyes was usually disastrous.

By the time Judges ends, Israel is a mess. There's no central leadership. The tribes are fighting each other. A civil war has nearly wiped out an entire tribe. The priesthood is corrupt. The people have largely forgotten who God is and what he's done for them. They desperately need something to change.

First Samuel is that change. It opens with the last and greatest of the judges—Samuel—and ends with the death of Israel's first king—Saul. In between, we watch God reshape his people from a loose confederation of tribes into a united kingdom under a king.

But here's the twist: the king the people demand isn't the king God ultimately wants to give them. That tension drives the entire book.

WHAT YOU'RE ABOUT TO READ

First Samuel breaks naturally into three major sections:

Samuel's Story (Chapters 1–7): The book begins with a heartbroken woman named Hannah praying desperately for a son. God answers her prayer, and that son—Samuel—becomes the pivotal figure who bridges the old era and the new. Samuel serves as prophet, priest, and judge, calling Israel back to faithfulness and leading them to victory over the Philistines. He's the last of one kind of leader and the one who will anoint the first of another kind.

Saul's Rise and Fall (Chapters 8–15): Israel demands a king "like all the other nations." It's not a request that pleases God or Samuel, but God grants it—and warns them what they're getting into. Saul enters the story as a tall, handsome, humble young man who seems perfect for the job. His early reign shows promise. But then something goes wrong. Small compromises become big failures. Self-reliance replaces trust in God. By chapter 15, God has rejected Saul as king—even though Saul will keep the throne for many more years.

David's Rise and Saul's Decline (Chapters 16–31): While Saul is still king, God sends Samuel to anoint a replacement—a shepherd boy named David, the youngest son of a man named Jesse. What follows is one of the most dramatic sections of the entire Bible. David kills Goliath. He becomes Saul's armor-bearer, then his son-in-law, then his greatest enemy. Saul spirals into jealousy, paranoia, and violence, hunting David across the wilderness for years. David has multiple chances to kill Saul but refuses to lift his hand against "the LORD's anointed." The book ends with Saul's tragic death on Mount Gilboa and David poised to finally receive the kingdom God promised him.

THE HEART OF THE MATTER

There's a verse near the middle of 1 Samuel that captures what the whole book is about. When Samuel goes to anoint David, he's initially impressed by David's older brother Eliab—tall, strong, kingly-looking. But God stops him: "Do not look at his appearance or at his physical stature, because I have refused him. For the LORD does not see as man sees; for man looks at the outward appearance, but the LORD looks at the heart."

That's the lens through which you need to read this entire book. Saul *looked* like a king. He was head and shoulders taller than anyone else in Israel. He was from a wealthy family. He had the appearance of leadership. But his heart wasn't right. When tested, he chose his own judgment over God's commands. He cared more about what people thought than what God wanted. He looked like everything a king should be, but inside he was hollow.

David didn't look like much of anything. He was the youngest of eight sons, so insignificant that his own father didn't bother to bring him in when Samuel came looking for the future king. He was a shepherd—not exactly a prestigious job. Nobody would have picked him out of a lineup as royal material. But God saw his heart. And that made all the difference.

WHY THIS MATTERS FOR YOU

You might be thinking, "Okay, but I'm not going to be king of anything. Why does this matter to me?" Because the same question God asked about Saul and David, he asks about you: What's going on in your heart?

It's easy to focus on outward stuff—how you look, what people think of you, whether you're popular or successful. Our culture is obsessed with appearances. We learn early to curate an image, to show people what we want them to see.

But God isn't scrolling your highlight reel. He's looking at what's underneath—the real you behind the filtered version. And that's good news. Because it means you don't have to be the tallest, the smartest, or the most likely to succeed. David wasn't any of those things. What he was—and what you can be—is someone whose heart is pointed toward God.

First Samuel is also a warning. Saul's story shows how easily things can go wrong when we trust ourselves instead of God, when we make decisions based on fear instead of faith, and when we let jealousy and insecurity drive our actions. Saul didn't start out as a villain. He started with promise and potential. But his heart wasn't anchored to God, and when the storms came, he drifted until he was completely lost.

The difference between Saul and David wasn't that David was perfect—he definitely wasn't, as 2 Samuel will make painfully clear. The difference was what they did when they failed. Saul made excuses. David repented. Saul blamed others. David owned his sin. Saul tried to protect his image. David threw himself on God's mercy.

That's the kind of heart God is looking for. Not perfection—

honesty. Not flawless performance—humble dependence.

BEFORE YOU START

As you read through this book, you're going to encounter some dark material. Violence, jealousy, betrayal, mental illness, massacre, suicide. The Bible doesn't sanitize human experience, and 1 Samuel shows us people at their worst as well as their best.

You're also going to meet some unforgettable characters: Hannah, whose desperate prayer opens the whole story; Eli, the well-meaning priest who failed to restrain his wicked sons; Jonathan, whose friendship with David sets the standard for loyalty; Abigail, whose wisdom saved lives; the witch of Endor, whose séance revealed Saul's doom.

But most of all, you're going to watch God work. Behind all the human drama—the political maneuvering, the battlefield victories, the wilderness chases—God is sovereignly moving his plan forward. He's raising up a king after his own heart. He's preparing the way for a dynasty that will eventually produce the Messiah.

The story of David doesn't end in 1 Samuel. It doesn't even end in 2 Samuel or 1 Kings. It ends in a stable in Bethlehem, David's hometown, where another unexpected king was born—one who didn't look like much either, but whose heart was perfectly aligned with his Father's.

That king is still looking for people whose hearts are fully his.

Maybe that's you.

Turn the page, and let's find out what God sees when he looks at the heart.

1

A PRAYER IN THE DARK

Before Harry Potter knew he was a wizard, he lived in a cupboard under the stairs. Every day he watched the Dursleys spoil his cousin Dudley with presents, praise, and second helpings of everything. Meanwhile, Harry got hand-me-down clothes, cold leftovers, and constant reminders that he was unwanted. He didn't belong. He wasn't really part of the family. And nobody seemed to care about his pain.

If you've read the books or seen the movies, you know how the story turns out—Harry discovers he's not ordinary at all. He's been special all along. But before the Hogwarts letter arrived, before he knew the truth about himself, Harry was just a lonely kid wondering why his life was so unfair while everyone around him seemed to have it so good.

The story of 1 Samuel begins with a woman who understood that feeling perfectly. Her name was Hannah, and her pain wasn't about being stuck in a cupboard—it was about something that mattered even more in the ancient world. She couldn't have children. And just like Harry before his letter came, she had to live every single day feeling invisible and unimportant, watching someone else have exactly what she desperately wanted.

But here's what makes Hannah's story so incredible: her pain became the doorway to one of the greatest turning points in Israel's history. The son she eventually had—a boy named Samuel—would change everything. He would be the last of the judges and the first of the great prophets. He would anoint Israel's first two kings. He would guide the nation through one of its most dangerous and transformative periods.

And it all started with a broken woman crying in the tabernacle, pouring out her heart to a God she wasn't sure was listening.

WHEN EVERYTHING HURTS

The book of 1 Samuel opens by introducing us to a man named Elkanah, who lived in the hill country of Ephraim, in a town called Ramah. He was a respectable guy from a good family—the kind of person whose ancestors get listed by name because they mattered. He was also faithful to God, making the trip to the tabernacle at Shiloh every year to worship and offer sacrifices.

But Elkanah had a problem: his family was a mess. Elkanah had two wives. (Yes, this happened in the ancient world, though it always led to disaster.) One wife was named Peninnah, and she had children—lots of them. The other wife was named Hannah, and she had none.

You need to understand something about the ancient world. A woman's value was often tied to whether she could have children. It wasn't right, but it was real. A woman without children felt like a failure. People assumed something was wrong with her, maybe even that God was punishing her. Childlessness wasn't just sad—it was shameful.

And Hannah had to live with this shame every single day, right next to a woman who had exactly what she wanted.

The text tells us that "the LORD had closed her womb." That's a hard sentence to read. It means Hannah's childlessness wasn't random bad luck—God himself had done this. We're not told why. We're just told that it was true.

But here's what made it unbearable: Peninnah wouldn't let Hannah forget it. Year after year, especially when the family went to Shiloh to worship, Peninnah would provoke Hannah, irritate her, and rub her face in it. The Bible doesn't record Peninnah's exact words, but we can imagine: little comments about how many kids she had to keep track of, fake-innocent questions about whether Hannah would ever be a "real" mother, reminders that she was giving Elkanah the children Hannah couldn't provide.

It was relentless. It was cruel. And it worked. Hannah would end up in tears, unable to eat, her heart shattered all over again. Even Elkanah's attempts to comfort her fell flat. "Hannah, why are you crying?" he asked. "Why won't you eat? Why are you so sad? Don't I mean more to you than ten sons?"

Elkanah meant well. He loved Hannah—the text makes that clear. But he didn't understand. He couldn't understand. He had children through Peninnah. His legacy was secure. He would never know what it felt like to be Hannah, to ache for something so deeply that it felt like a hole in your chest that nothing could fill.

A DESPERATE PRAYER

One year at Shiloh, after the sacrificial meal, Hannah couldn't take it anymore. She got up and went to the tabernacle—the tent where God's presence dwelt among his people. The old priest Eli was sitting by the doorpost, probably half-asleep after the feast.

Hannah began to pray. But this wasn't a polite, formal prayer. This was something raw and broken. She was "deeply distressed" and "wept bitterly." She was pouring out her soul before God, not with elegant words but with desperate ones.

And she made a vow: "O LORD of hosts, if you will look on the affliction of your servant and remember me, and not forget your servant, but will give your servant a son, then I will give him to the LORD all the days of his life, and no razor shall touch his head."

Think about what she's promising. She's not asking for a son so she can finally win against Peninnah. She's not asking for a child so she can feel complete. She's asking for a son—and promising to give him right back to God. If God would only remember her, only see her, only give her this one thing, she would dedicate that child to the Lord forever.

The "no razor" part was a reference to something called a Nazirite vow—a special dedication to God that meant the person would be set apart for holy purposes. Hannah was offering her future son to God before he even existed.

Here's what's remarkable: Hannah was praying to the same God who had closed her womb. She wasn't angry at God (or if she was, she brought that anger to him honestly). She didn't turn away from him because of her pain. Instead, she ran toward him. She trusted that the God who had allowed her suffering was also the only one who could end it.

Meanwhile, old Eli watched her. He saw her lips moving but couldn't hear any words—Hannah was praying silently, from her heart. Eli jumped to the wrong conclusion. "How long will you keep on being drunk?" he demanded. "Put away your wine!"

Great. The one religious leader around, and he mistakes desperate prayer for drunkenness. This is actually a clue about how bad things had gotten in Israel. Even the high priest couldn't recognize genuine spiritual passion when he saw it.

Hannah corrected him gently: "No, my lord, I am a woman troubled in spirit. I have not been drinking. I have been pouring out my soul before the LORD."

Something in her words got through to Eli. His tone changed completely. "Go in peace," he said, "and may the God of Israel grant you what you have asked of him."

And then something changed in Hannah. The text says she "went her way and ate, and her face was no longer sad." She hadn't received anything yet—no baby, no guarantee, no sign from heaven. But something had shifted. She had brought her pain to God, and somehow that was enough. She could trust him with the outcome.

THE BOY WHO CHANGED EVERYTHING

God remembered Hannah. Those three words are packed with meaning. In the Bible, when God "remembers" someone, it doesn't mean he had forgotten them. It means he's about to act on their behalf. He's about to move.

Hannah conceived and gave birth to a son. She named him Samuel, which sounds like the Hebrew words for "heard by God." Every time she said his name, she was remembering: *God heard me. God answered. God remembered.*

But Hannah didn't forget her vow. When Samuel was old enough to be weaned—probably around three years old—she took him to the tabernacle at Shiloh. She brought offerings: a three-year-old bull, flour, and wine. She found Eli and reminded him of their encounter: "I am the woman who was standing here, praying to the LORD. For this child I prayed, and the LORD has granted me my petition. Therefore I have lent him to the LORD. As long as he lives, he is lent to the LORD."

Imagine doing that. Imagine waiting years for a child, finally holding him in your arms, watching him grow from infant to toddler, hearing his first words, seeing his first steps—and then handing him over. Walking away. Leaving your miracle child at the tabernacle to be raised by someone else.

Hannah did it. Not because it was easy, but because she had made a promise to God, and she intended to keep it.

Before she left, Hannah prayed again. This prayer is recorded in 1 Samuel 2, and it's completely different from her first one. The first prayer was all tears and desperation. This one is all praise and prophecy. Hannah celebrates the God who "brings low and exalts," who "raises up the poor from the dust."

And then she says something surprising: "The LORD will judge the ends of the earth; he will give strength to his king and exalt the horn of his anointed."

Wait—his king? His anointed? Israel didn't have a king yet. But Hannah's prayer looks forward to the day when God would raise up a king for his people. Her son Samuel would be the one to anoint that king. Hannah was prophesying without even knowing it.

GROWING UP IN A BROKEN PLACE

Little Samuel stayed at Shiloh, serving the Lord under Eli's supervision. Every year, Hannah would visit and bring him a new robe she had made. And God blessed Hannah with more children—three sons and two daughters.

But Samuel wasn't growing up in a good environment. Shiloh should have been the holiest place in Israel—the location of the tabernacle, the center of worship. Instead, it was corrupt.

Eli's two sons, Hophni and Phinehas, were priests. But they were also, as the Bible bluntly puts it, "worthless men." They treated the sacrifices with contempt, taking the best meat for themselves before it was even offered to God. They slept with women who served at the tabernacle entrance. They used their position for personal gain instead of serving the people.

Old Eli knew about it. He even confronted his sons—sort of. But when they ignored him, he didn't do anything about it. He was weak. He let it continue. He honored his sons more than he honored God.

Meanwhile, young Samuel "continued to grow both in stature and in favor with the LORD and also with man." In the middle of all this corruption, one boy was different.

A VOICE IN THE NIGHT

Then came the night that changed everything. The text sets the scene with a haunting detail: "The word of the LORD was rare in those days; there was no frequent vision." God had gone quiet. Maybe it was because of the corruption at Shiloh. Maybe it was part of his plan. Either way, people weren't hearing from God anymore. The lamp of God hadn't yet gone out—it was still burning in the tabernacle—but dawn was coming. Something was about to shift.

Samuel was lying down in the tabernacle, near the ark of God. Eli was in his usual place, his eyesight nearly gone. Then Samuel heard his name.

"Samuel!"

He jumped up and ran to Eli. "Here I am, for you called me."

But Eli hadn't called him. "I did not call; lie down again."

Samuel went back to bed. Then it happened again.

"Samuel!"

Again he ran to Eli. Again Eli sent him back. "I did not call, my son; lie down again."

Now here's an important detail: "Samuel did not yet know the LORD, and the word of the LORD had not yet been revealed to him." This doesn't mean Samuel didn't believe in God. It means he had never experienced God speaking directly to him. He didn't recognize the voice.

It happened a third time. Samuel heard his name, ran to Eli, and said, "Here I am, for you called me."

Finally, Eli figured it out. Despite all his failures, the old priest understood what was happening. "Go, lie down," he told Samuel, "and if he calls you, you shall say, 'Speak, LORD, for your servant is listening.'"

Samuel went back and lay down. And then God came. The

text says the LORD came and stood there, calling as before, "Samuel! Samuel!"

This time, Samuel answered correctly: "Speak, for your servant is listening."

What happened next was terrifying. God told Samuel that he was about to do something in Israel that would make the ears of everyone who heard it tingle. He was going to judge the house of Eli—completely, finally, irreversibly. Eli knew his sons were blaspheming God, and he didn't stop them. Now judgment was coming, and no sacrifice or offering would ever make it right.

Imagine being a boy—maybe twelve years old—and receiving a message like that. A message of doom for the man who had raised you. A message that would shatter your mentor's world.

Samuel lay there until morning, afraid to tell Eli what he had heard. He got up and opened the doors of the tabernacle like normal, going through the motions, dreading the conversation he knew was coming.

But Eli wouldn't let it go. "Samuel, my son," he called. Then he pressed him: "What was it that he told you? Do not hide it from me. May God do so to you and more also if you hide anything from me of all that he told you."

So Samuel told him everything. He didn't hold back a single word. And Eli's response is both heartbreaking and noble: "It is the LORD. Let him do what seems good to him."

No arguing. No excuses. No bargaining. Just acceptance. Whatever else was wrong with Eli, in this moment he bowed before God's judgment and accepted it.

A PROPHET FOR ALL ISRAEL

From that night on, everything was different. Samuel grew, and the Lord was with him. None of Samuel's words fell to the ground—meaning everything he prophesied came true. Word spread throughout the land, from Dan in the north to Beer-sheba in the south: Samuel was the real deal. He was a true prophet of the Lord.

For the first time in a long time, God was speaking to his people again. And he was doing it through a boy who had been born to a barren woman, dedicated before his birth, and raised in a broken, corrupt place.

The lamp of God had been flickering. But it didn't go out. Samuel was the spark that would eventually become a fire.

WHAT THIS MEANS FOR US

So what do we take away from this opening act of 1 Samuel?

First, God works through overlooked people. Hannah was a childless woman in a world that valued women primarily for having children. She was mocked and dismissed. But God saw her. God heard her. And God used her pain to launch one of the most important ministries in Israel's history. If you've ever felt invisible, Hannah's story reminds you that God's view of you is very different from the world's.

Second, desperate prayers get God's attention. Hannah didn't pray polite, careful prayers. She poured out her soul. She was messy and raw. And God answered. Sometimes we think our prayers need to be perfect and organized. Hannah shows us that God welcomes broken honesty more than polished performance.

Third, God is patient with people who are learning. When God called Samuel, the boy didn't recognize his voice. It took three tries before Samuel figured out what was happening. But God didn't get frustrated. He kept calling until Samuel was ready to listen. If you feel like you're slow to understand what God is doing in your life, take heart. He's patient with learners.

Fourth, faithfulness matters more than circumstances. Samuel grew up surrounded by corruption. Hophni and Phinehas were terrible examples. But Samuel didn't become like them. He stayed faithful. Your environment doesn't have to determine your character.

Fifth, God's silence doesn't mean God's absence. The word of the Lord was "rare" in Samuel's early years. But God wasn't gone—he was preparing something. Sometimes the quiet seasons are the setup for the next breakthrough.

TALKING POINTS

Here are some things to think about and discuss:

1. **Hannah's rival, Peninnah, constantly provoked her about not having children.** Why do you think people sometimes hurt others who are already struggling? How should we respond when someone is cruel to us?

2. **Elkanah tried to comfort Hannah by asking, "Am I not more to you than ten sons?"** Why wasn't that helpful? What do people sometimes say when they're trying to help that actually doesn't help?

3. **Hannah promised to give her son back to God before he was even born.** What do you think that tells us about her

faith? Could you give away something you desperately wanted, just because you promised God you would?

4. **Samuel didn't recognize God's voice at first.** What are some ways God might speak to people today? How can we get better at recognizing when God is trying to get our attention?

5. **Samuel grew up surrounded by corrupt priests, but he didn't become like them.** What helps a person stay faithful when everyone around them is making bad choices?

The story of Samuel's birth and calling is really about two things: God's power to bring something out of nothing, and God's habit of choosing unlikely people for impossible tasks.

Hannah had nothing—no children, no hope, no status. But she had faith, and that faith connected her to a God who specializes in turning emptiness into abundance.

Samuel was just a boy—inexperienced, growing up in a corrupt place. But he was available, and God can do a lot with someone who's available.

The lamp of God was still burning. The voice of God was about to be heard again. And Israel would never be the same.

Turn the page.

2

THE ARK STRIKES BACK

In *Raiders of the Lost Ark*, Indiana Jones spends the entire movie trying to find the Ark of the Covenant before the Nazis can get their hands on it. The ark is the most powerful artifact in history, and whoever controls it—according to the legend—will have an unstoppable army. The Nazis finally capture it, take it to a secret island, and open it in a grand ceremony, expecting to receive unimaginable power. Instead, they get melted.

The ark isn't a weapon you can aim. It isn't a tool you can use. It's holy—and when unholy people try to treat it like their personal power source, very bad things happen.

Thousands of years before that movie was made, the people of Israel learned the same lesson. And so did the Philistines. In 1 Samuel 4–7, we see what happens when people treat God like a good luck charm, a magic box, or a cosmic vending machine. Spoiler alert: it doesn't go well for anyone.

But we also see something else—something beautiful. We see what happens when people finally stop trying to use God and start actually following him. We see repentance. We see rescue. We see the moment when Israel finally gets it right.

And we see a stone monument called Ebenezer—a marker that reminds God's people of a simple but life-changing truth: "Thus far the LORD has helped us."

WHEN GOD BECOMES A GOOD LUCK CHARM

The Philistines were bad news. They had settled along the coast of Canaan, and they were constantly pushing inland, trying to take more territory. They had better weapons than Israel (they knew how to work with iron, which was a big deal back then), better organization, and a lot of military confidence.

Israel went out to fight them and got crushed. Four thousand Israelite soldiers died in a single battle near a place called Aphek. When the survivors staggered back to camp, the elders of Israel asked exactly the right question: "Why did the LORD bring defeat upon us today?"

That was the right question. They understood that God was in control of the outcome. They recognized that their defeat wasn't random—it had something to do with their relationship with God.

But then they gave exactly the wrong answer. Instead of asking, "Have we sinned? Have we turned away from God? Is there something in our lives that needs to change?"—they came up with a different plan: "Let's go get the ark of the covenant from Shiloh! If we bring the ark into battle, God will have to help us. We'll win for sure!"

You need to understand what the ark was. It was a gold-covered wooden box that sat in the Most Holy Place of the tabernacle, the innermost part of God's dwelling place among his people. On top of the ark were two golden angels called cherubim, and between them was what the Bible calls the "mercy seat"—the place where God's presence rested. The ark contained the stone tablets with the Ten Commandments, and it represented God's throne on earth.

The ark had been at the center of some of Israel's greatest moments. When Israel crossed the Jordan River into the Promised Land, the priests carried the ark ahead of them, and the waters parted. When Israel marched around Jericho, the ark led the way and the walls fell down. The ark was the visible symbol of God's presence and power.

So you can see why the elders thought bringing the ark to battle was a good idea. If God's presence goes with us, we can't lose! Right?

Wrong.

Here's what the elders got backwards: they thought the ark would force God to fight for them. They thought having God's furniture meant having God's power. They were treating the ark like a magic object—like a rabbit's foot or a lucky charm. Rub it the right way, and good things happen.

But God isn't a force you can control by having the right stuff. He's not a genie in a lamp. He's not a power source you can plug into whenever you need a boost. He's the living God, and he will not be manipulated.

THE DAY EVERYTHING FELL APART

They sent for the ark. Eli's two corrupt sons, Hophni and Phinehas, came with it. When the ark arrived in the Israelite camp, the soldiers let out a shout so loud that the ground shook. They were pumped. Victory was certain now!

The Philistines heard the shouting and got nervous. "A god has come into their camp!" they said. "We're in trouble! These are the gods who struck the Egyptians with plagues!" (They had the story a bit garbled, but they had the right idea—Israel's God was powerful.)

But the Philistine commanders rallied their troops: "Be strong! Be men! Fight hard, or you'll become slaves to the Hebrews!"

And then came the battle. And Israel lost. Badly. Thirty thousand Israelite soldiers died that day. The army scattered. Hophni and Phinehas were killed. And the unthinkable happened: the Philistines captured the ark of God.

Think about what this meant. The most sacred object in Israel—the symbol of God's presence, the throne of the Almighty—was now in the hands of pagan enemies. To anyone watching, it looked like Israel's God had been defeated. It looked like he couldn't protect his own stuff.

But that's not what happened at all. God wasn't defeated. He let the ark be captured. He allowed it because his own people had tried to use him, and he would rather suffer shame than let them continue in their false religion. He let them be disappointed with him so they might finally wake up and understand who he really is.

THE GLORY HAS DEPARTED

Back at Shiloh, ninety-eight-year-old Eli sat by the road, waiting for news. He couldn't see anymore—his eyes had grown too weak. But his heart was pounding. He was terrified about what might have happened to the ark.

A messenger came running from the battle, his clothes torn and dirt on his head—the ancient way of showing grief and disaster. When he reached the city and told the news, the whole town erupted in wailing.

Eli heard the noise. "What's going on?" he asked. The messenger came to him and delivered the news piece by piece, like hammer blows: Israel fled. There was a great slaughter. Your two sons, Hophni and Phinehas, are dead. And the ark of God has been captured.

At those last words—"the ark of God has been captured"—Eli fell backward off his seat. He was old and heavy. His neck broke, and he died.

Eli had judged Israel for forty years. His failures had led to this moment—his refusal to restrain his wicked sons, his weakness, his willingness to let corruption continue under his watch. Now it was over.

But there's one more scene. Eli's daughter-in-law, the wife of Phinehas, was pregnant. When she heard that the ark was captured and that her husband and father-in-law were dead, she went into labor. The birth went badly, and she was dying.

The women around her tried to comfort her: "Don't be afraid! You've had a son!"

But she didn't respond. She didn't care. With her last breath, she named the baby Ichabod, which means "no glory" or "the glory has departed." Then she died. "The glory has departed from Israel," she said, "for the ark of God has been captured."

This is one of the darkest moments in the entire Old Testament. The leadership is dead. The ark is gone. The glory has departed. It looks like the end of everything.

But it wasn't. Because even when Israel's faith failed, God was still God.

THE ARK FIGHTS BACK

The Philistines took the ark to Ashdod, one of their main cities, and placed it in the temple of their god Dagon as a trophy. Dagon was a major Philistine deity, and putting the ark in his temple was a way of saying, "Our god beat your god."

The next morning, the Philistines came into the temple and found Dagon's statue lying face-down in front of the ark. It looked like Dagon was bowing to Israel's God. They set the statue back up.

The next morning, Dagon was face-down again—but this time his head and hands had broken off. The idol was in pieces at the threshold of its own temple.

Then things got worse. The people of Ashdod started breaking out in painful tumors. The whole city was in an uproar. "The ark of Israel's God can't stay here," they said. "His hand is heavy on us and on Dagon our god."

So they sent the ark to Gath. Same thing—tumors everywhere, panic in the streets.

They sent it to Ekron. The people of Ekron saw it coming and started screaming: "Don't bring that thing here! It's going to kill us all!"

For seven months the ark moved from city to city, and everywhere it went, disaster followed. The Philistines who had captured the ark of God were now desperate to get rid of it. They called their priests and diviners and asked, "What do we do? How do we send this thing back?"

The answer was elaborate: put the ark on a new cart pulled by two cows that had never been yoked. Send along gold offerings as a guilt payment. Then let the cows go wherever they want. If they head toward Israel, you'll know that Israel's God really did this to us. If not, maybe it was all coincidence.

The cows headed straight for Israel, never turning aside, mooing the whole way. The Philistine rulers followed at a distance, watching. When the cart arrived at Beth Shemesh, an Israelite town, the people were overjoyed. They sacrificed the cows as burnt offerings and celebrated.

But then some of the men of Beth Shemesh looked inside the ark—something strictly forbidden. Seventy of them died. The people were terrified. "Who can stand in the presence of the LORD, this holy God?" they cried.

They sent the ark to Kiriath Jearim, where it stayed at the house of a man named Abinadab for twenty years. The ark was back in Israel, but things weren't right yet. The people still hadn't dealt with their real problem.

THE TURNING POINT

Twenty years passed. The Philistines still dominated Israel. The people were miserable, mourning and longing for God. And finally—finally—they were ready to listen.

Samuel, now grown and established as a prophet, spoke to the nation: "If you are returning to the LORD with all your hearts, then get rid of the foreign gods and the Ashtoreths among you. Commit yourselves to the LORD and serve him only, and he will deliver you from the Philistines."

This was the moment of truth. For generations, Israel had

been worshiping the gods of the nations around them alongside the LORD. They wanted God's blessings, but they also wanted to keep their idols. They wanted heaven's protection without heaven's standards.

Samuel said that was over. It was time to choose. And this time, Israel listened. They put away their foreign gods. They gathered at Mizpah, where Samuel called them to fast and confess their sins. They poured out water before the Lord—a symbol of pouring out their hearts in repentance. "We have sinned against the LORD," they said.

Real repentance isn't just feeling bad. It's actually turning around—getting rid of the things that have been pulling you away from God and committing to go a different direction. Israel finally did that.

THUNDER FROM HEAVEN

When the Philistines heard that Israel had gathered at Mizpah, they saw an opportunity. A large religious assembly meant the Israelites were in one place, probably unarmed, easy targets. The Philistine army marched.

When Israel saw the Philistine forces coming, they were terrified. They begged Samuel, "Don't stop crying out to the LORD our God for us! Ask him to rescue us from the Philistines!"

This was different from before. Before, they had trusted in the ark—in having the right object. Now they were trusting in God himself. They were asking Samuel to pray, not to produce a magic charm.

Samuel took a young lamb and offered it as a burnt offering. As he was sacrificing, the Philistine army approached for battle. And then God acted.

The Lord thundered with a mighty sound against the Philistines that day. It wasn't just a storm—it was divine intervention, unmistakable and terrifying. The Philistines panicked. Their ranks dissolved into confusion. They ran.

The Israelites came out of Mizpah and chased the Philistines, striking them down all the way to Beth Car. It was a complete victory—not because Israel had better weapons or superior tactics, but because God fought for them.

What made the difference? Not the ark. Not religious rituals. Not organizational strategies. The difference was repentance. The difference was turning back to God with their whole hearts.

THE STONE OF HELP

After the battle, Samuel did something important. He took a large stone and set it up between Mizpah and Shen as a monument. He named it Ebenezer, which means "stone of help." "Thus far the LORD has helped us," Samuel declared.

Think about that name. Years earlier, at a place also called Ebenezer, Israel had suffered a devastating defeat. They had lost the ark. They had lost thirty thousand men. They had lost Eli and his sons. They had lost everything.

Now, at this new Ebenezer, everything had been restored. The Philistines were subdued. The territories they had taken were returned to Israel. Peace came to the land.

Samuel's monument was a reminder: "Look how far God has brought us. Remember what he's done." The same God who let them fail when they tried to use him was the God who rescued them when they truly turned to him.

That phrase—"Thus far the LORD has helped us"—is one of the most important sentences in the Old Testament. It's a statement that looks backward and forward at the same time. Backward: remember all the ways God has helped you. Forward: if he has helped you this far, he will help you the rest of the way.

Samuel went on to judge Israel for the rest of his life. He traveled a regular circuit—Bethel, Gilgal, Mizpah—settling disputes and teaching the people. He built an altar at his hometown of Ramah. The period of chaos was over. A new era had begun.

WHAT THIS MEANS FOR US

So what do we take from these dramatic chapters?

First, God won't be used. The Israelites tried to turn God into a good luck charm. They thought having the ark meant having power. But God isn't a tool in our toolkit. He isn't a force we can harness for our own purposes. When we try to use God—when we treat prayer like a magic spell or church attendance like a loyalty card that earns us points—we've made the same mistake Israel made.

Second, hitting bottom can be the beginning of healing. Israel had to lose everything before they were willing to change. The ark had to be captured, Eli had to die, twenty years of Philistine domination had to pass before the people were finally ready to repent. Sometimes God lets us fail so we'll finally look up.

Third, real repentance requires real action. Samuel didn't tell Israel to just feel sorry for their sins. He told them to get rid of their idols. He told them to commit to the Lord alone. Repentance isn't just an emotion—it's a direction change. It means actually removing the things that have been pulling you away from God.

Fourth, God responds to genuine returning. When Israel finally came back to God for real—not with tricks or manipulation, but with humble, whole-hearted repentance—God showed up in power. The thunder that routed the Philistines was God's answer to a people who had finally stopped playing games.

Fifth, we need our own Ebenezer stones. Samuel's monument was a permanent reminder of what God had done. We need those too—ways of remembering God's faithfulness so we don't forget. Maybe it's a journal where you record answered prayers. Maybe it's a tradition of telling stories about how God has worked in your family. Maybe it's simply pausing to say "thank you" when you realize how far God has brought you.

TALKING POINTS

1. **Israel tried to use the ark like a magic object to guarantee victory.** What are some ways people today try to "use" God or treat religion like a good luck charm?

2. **When the ark was captured, it looked like God had been defeated.** But was he? What was God actually doing by letting the ark be taken?

3. **The Philistines experienced disaster after disaster while the ark was in their territory.** What do you think this taught them about Israel's God compared to their own gods?

4. **Israel had to wait twenty years before things turned around.** Why do you think God made them wait so long? What might have been happening in their hearts during that time?

5. **Samuel set up a stone and called it "Ebenezer"—stone of help.** What are some "Ebenezer moments" in your own life or your family's life—times when God clearly helped you that you want to remember?

The ark adventure teaches us something crucial about how God works: he won't be manipulated, but he loves to be trusted. He won't be controlled, but he delights to rescue those who genuinely turn to him.

Israel tried the manipulation route. It failed spectacularly. They lost everything—including, for a time, the very symbol of God's presence among them. But when they finally came back with humble hearts and empty hands, ready to serve God on his terms instead of theirs, everything changed. The thunder rolled. The enemies fled. The stone was raised. Thus far the Lord has helped us. And he's not done yet.

Turn the page.

3

BE CAREFUL WHAT YOU WISH FOR

In *The Little Mermaid*, Ariel wants something so badly she can taste it: legs. She wants to walk on land, to be part of the human world, to fit in with the people she's been watching from the sea. When Ursula the sea witch offers her a deal—her voice in exchange for legs—Ariel doesn't hesitate. She signs the contract without reading the fine print, without considering the consequences, without asking her father or anyone who might have warned her what she was really giving up.

And it nearly destroys her.

Ariel got what she wanted. But getting what you want isn't always the same as getting what you need. Sometimes the thing you're desperate for comes with costs you never imagined. Sometimes your wish, once granted, becomes your worst nightmare.

In 1 Samuel 8–12, the people of Israel are about to make the same kind of deal. They want a king—desperately. They want to be like the other nations. They want someone tall and impressive to lead them into battle. And God, after warning them repeatedly about what this will cost, gives them exactly what they asked for.

Be careful what you wish for. You might just get it.

THE DEMAND

Samuel had grown old. His hair was gray, his steps were slower, and everyone knew he wouldn't be around forever. This was a problem because Samuel had been the glue holding Israel together—prophet, priest, judge, and intercessor all rolled into one.

To prepare for the future, Samuel appointed his two sons, Joel and Abijah, as judges in Beersheba. It seemed like a reasonable plan. The problem was that Samuel's sons were nothing like their father. They were corrupt. They took bribes. They twisted justice for personal gain. They were, in fact, a lot like Eli's sons had been—and everyone remembered how that had turned out.

So the elders of Israel gathered and came to Samuel at Ramah. They had a proposal. "Look," they said, "you're old, and your sons don't follow your ways. Appoint a king to lead us, like all the other nations have."

On the surface, this seemed perfectly reasonable. Samuel was aging. His sons were corrupt. The current system wasn't working. A king would provide stable leadership, military strength, and national unity. Every other nation had one. Why shouldn't Israel?

But Samuel knew something was wrong with this request. He could feel it. The demand for a king "displeased" him—not because kings were forbidden (God had actually made provision for kings in Deuteronomy 17), but because of what was behind the request.

Samuel prayed. And God gave him a devastating answer. "Listen to them," God said. "But understand what's really happening here. They haven't rejected you, Samuel. They've rejected me. They don't want me as their king anymore. This is what they've always done—from the day I brought them out of Egypt until now. They keep abandoning me and serving other gods. Now they're doing it to you too."

Did you catch that? The problem wasn't that Israel wanted a king. The problem was why they wanted one. They weren't looking for a leader who would help them follow God better. They were looking for a replacement for God. They wanted to trust in a human king instead of trusting in the Lord. They wanted to be "like all the other nations"—which was exactly what Israel was never supposed to be.

Think about it this way: when Israel faced enemies in the past, they cried out to God, and he sent deliverers. That's what happened with Moses. That's what happened with the judges. The pattern was: trouble comes, Israel prays, God rescues.

But this time, when the Ammonite king Nahash started threatening them, Israel didn't cry out to God. They demanded a king. They wanted a military solution, not a spiritual one. They wanted to fix their problems with better government instead of dealing with their hearts.

God told Samuel to warn them. Tell them what having a king will really cost.

THE WARNING

So Samuel laid it out. He told the people exactly what life under a king would look like, and it wasn't pretty. "This is what the king who reigns over you will do," Samuel said. "He will take your sons and make them serve with his chariots and horses. They'll run in front of his chariots. He'll assign some to be commanders, others to plow his fields, and others to make weapons and military equipment.

"He will take your daughters to be perfumers, cooks, and bakers. He will take the best of your fields, your vineyards, your olive groves, and give them to his officials. He will take a tenth of your grain and wine and give it to his servants. He will take your male and female servants, your best cattle and donkeys, and use them for his own purposes. He will take a tenth of your flocks. And you—you yourselves—will become his slaves.

"When that day comes, you will cry out for relief from the king you have chosen. But the LORD will not answer you in that day."

Notice the repeated word: take, take, take, take, take. That's what kings do. That's what power does. Samuel wasn't describing a worst-case scenario—he was describing what normal kings were like in the ancient world. They drafted your sons into their armies. They taxed your crops. They claimed your property. They turned free people into servants of the state.

God was offering Israel something different—a theocracy, where God himself was king and his people lived in freedom under his rule. But Israel wanted to trade that freedom for a human monarch. They wanted to be like everyone else.

And here's the heartbreaking part: even after this warning, they didn't care. "No!" they said. "We want a king over us. Then we'll be like all the other nations, with a king to lead us and go out before us and fight our battles."

They heard the warning. They understood the cost. And they wanted it anyway.

God told Samuel to give them what they asked for.

THE UNLIKELY KING

The next scene is almost comical. We meet Saul, son of Kish, from the tribe of Benjamin. The text tells us two things about him right away: he was "an impressive young man," and he was taller than anyone else in Israel—"a head taller than any of the others."

Saul wasn't out looking for a kingdom. He was looking for his father's lost donkeys. He and a servant had been searching for days without success when they decided to consult a prophet who might be able to help. That prophet turned out to be Samuel.

But God had already told Samuel that Saul was coming. "About this time tomorrow," God said, "I will send you a man from the land of Benjamin. Anoint him ruler over my people Israel. He will deliver them from the Philistines."

When Samuel saw Saul, God confirmed it: "This is the man I spoke to you about. He will govern my people."

Saul was confused. He had come looking for donkeys, and suddenly this prophet was treating him like royalty—giving him the best seat at a feast, the choicest portion of meat, and then, the next morning, anointing his head with oil and telling him he would be Israel's first king. "The LORD has anointed you ruler over his inheritance," Samuel said.

To confirm this wasn't all a dream, Samuel gave Saul a series of signs that would happen on his way home—and every single one came true. When Saul met a group of prophets, the Spirit of God came upon him powerfully, and he prophesied along with them. People who knew him were stunned: "What happened to Saul? Is Saul actually among the prophets?" Saul had been transformed. He was given "a new heart." God was with him.

But there were warning signs even here. When Saul got home and his uncle asked where he'd been, Saul mentioned meeting Samuel and learning about the donkeys—but he didn't say a word about being anointed king. He kept it secret. Was he humble? Was he afraid? Was he not quite sure he wanted this? We don't know. But it's an odd silence for a man just told he would lead an entire nation.

HIDING IN THE BAGGAGE

Samuel called all Israel together at Mizpah for a public selection of the king. He reminded them, one more time, of what they were doing: "You have rejected your God, who saves you out of all your disasters and calamities. And you have said, 'No, appoint a king over us.'"

Then Samuel used the sacred lots to narrow down the selection—first to the tribe of Benjamin, then to the clan of Matri, then finally to Saul son of Kish.

But when they went to bring Saul forward, he was nowhere to be found. "Has the man come here?" they asked the Lord.

"Yes," God said. "He's hidden himself among the baggage."

They ran and dragged him out. There he stood—tall, handsome, impressive—hiding among the supplies because he didn't want to be king.

Samuel presented him to the people: "Do you see the man the LORD has chosen? There is no one like him among all the people." And the people shouted, "Long live the king!"

Some people were excited. Others were skeptical. "How can this fellow save us?" some scoundrels muttered. They despised Saul and brought him no gifts.

Saul went home to Gibeah, accompanied by valiant men whose hearts God had touched. He didn't immediately try to establish his throne or punish his critics. He just went back to farming. It was an uncertain beginning for Israel's first king.

THE TEST

Saul's first real test came about a month later. Nahash the Ammonite attacked the city of Jabesh Gilead in the territory east of the Jordan. The people of Jabesh tried to negotiate a treaty, but Nahash's terms were horrifying: "I will make a treaty with you only on the condition that I gouge out the right eye of every one of you." This wasn't just cruelty—it was humiliation. It was meant to disgrace all of Israel.

When messengers brought this news to Gibeah, the people wept. Saul was coming in from the fields with his oxen when he heard the commotion. "What's wrong with everyone?" he asked.

When they told him what Nahash had threatened, something happened. The Spirit of God came upon Saul in power. His anger burned hot. He took a pair of oxen, cut them into pieces, and sent the pieces throughout Israel with a message: "This is what will be done to the oxen of anyone who doesn't follow Saul and Samuel."

The terror of the LORD fell on the people, and they came out as one man—330,000 soldiers from Israel and Judah.

Saul organized the army into three divisions. They attacked the Ammonite camp at dawn and slaughtered them until the heat of the day. The victory was total. The threat was eliminated. Israel was saved.

Now the people were excited. "Who was it that asked, 'Shall Saul reign over us?' Turn these men over to us so we can put them to death!"

But Saul refused. "No one will be put to death today," he said, "for this day the LORD has rescued Israel."

It was Saul's finest moment—victorious in battle, generous in triumph, giving credit to God. For one shining day, it looked like Israel's gamble on a king might actually work out.

SAMUEL'S FAREWELL

After the victory, Samuel gathered the people at Gilgal to "reaffirm the kingship." But Samuel had something to say first—something Israel needed to hear.

He began by defending his own integrity. "I have walked before you from my youth until this day. Here I am. Testify against me before the LORD. Whose ox have I taken? Whose donkey? Whom have I cheated? Whom have I oppressed? From whose hand have I accepted a bribe?"

"You have not cheated or oppressed us," the people replied. "You have not taken anything from anyone's hand."

Samuel had led Israel faithfully. He had nothing to hide. Now he turned to confront the people about their choice.

He walked them through their history—how God had delivered them from Egypt, how God had raised up judges whenever they repented, how God had always been faithful even when they were faithless. The pattern was clear: when Israel trusted God, they were rescued. When they abandoned him, they suffered.

"But when you saw that Nahash king of the Ammonites was moving against you," Samuel said, "you said to me, 'No, we want a king to rule over us'—even though the LORD your God was your king."

Then Samuel did something dramatic. It was wheat harvest—the driest time of year, when rain simply didn't come. Samuel said, "Now watch this great thing the LORD is about to do. I will call on the LORD to send thunder and rain. Then you will realize what an evil thing you did in the eyes of the LORD when you asked for a king."

Samuel prayed. And God sent thunder and rain. The people were terrified. A storm during wheat harvest? This was God answering Samuel's prayer, confirming every word he had spoken. Israel had sinned. They had demanded a king when they should have trusted their God. "Pray to the LORD your God for us," they begged Samuel, "so that we will not die! We have added to all our other sins the evil of asking for a king."

GRACE GREATER THAN SIN

Here's where the story takes a beautiful turn. Samuel had every right to say, "I told you so." He had every right to leave them in their terror. Instead, he pointed them back to grace.

"Don't be afraid," Samuel said. "You have done all this evil. But don't turn away from the LORD. Serve him with all your heart. Don't turn aside after useless idols. They can't help you or rescue you—they are nothing. For the sake of his great name, the LORD will not reject his people, because the LORD was pleased to make you his own."

Did you catch that? Even after all their sin—even after rejecting God as their king—God would not reject them. His commitment to Israel wasn't based on their faithfulness. It was based on his name, his character, his promise.

Samuel made his own commitment: "As for me, far be it from me that I should sin against the LORD by failing to pray for you. I will teach you the way that is good and right."

Then the warning: "But if you persist in doing evil, both you and your king will be swept away."

Israel had their king. The era of the judges was over. A new chapter had begun—one filled with both promise and danger.

WHAT THIS MEANS FOR US

First, wanting to be like everyone else is spiritually dangerous. Israel's demand to be "like all the nations" was a rejection of their unique calling. God had set them apart, made them different for a reason. When we chase conformity—when fitting in matters more than faithfulness—we make the same mistake Israel made.

Second, God sometimes gives us what we ask for as a form of judgment. Israel wanted a king. God gave them one. But getting what we want isn't always a blessing. Sometimes it's a warning. Sometimes God lets us have our way so we can learn why his way was better.

Third, the real problem is usually in our hearts, not our systems. Israel thought better government would fix their problems. But their real problem was spiritual—they had stopped trusting God. New structures can't fix old hearts.

Fourth, God's grace is bigger than our worst mistakes. Even after Israel's sin, God didn't abandon them. "The LORD will not reject his people." That's grace. We can't out-sin God's commitment to those he loves.

Fifth, leaders matter, but they can't save us. Saul looked like everything Israel wanted—tall, impressive, victorious. But he was still just a man. Every human leader will eventually disappoint. Only one King will never fail.

TALKING POINTS

1. **Israel wanted a king "like all the other nations."** Why is the desire to fit in and be like everyone else so powerful? What are some ways people your age feel that pressure today?

2. **Samuel warned Israel about what a king would "take" from them.** Why do you think they still wanted one? Have you ever wanted something so badly you ignored the warnings?

3. **Saul was found hiding among the baggage when he was supposed to be presented as king.** What do you think was going on in his mind? Is hiding from responsibility ever the right choice?

4. **Samuel defended his integrity before Israel—he had never cheated or taken bribes.** Why is it important for leaders to have that kind of record? How can we build that kind of integrity in our own lives?

5. **After all Israel's sin, Samuel said God would "not reject his people."** How does it feel to know that God's commitment to us doesn't depend on our perfect behavior?

Israel got their king. They got what they wished for. The question now was whether it would be a blessing or a curse.

The answer, as we'll see, is complicated. Saul started strong. But the seeds of failure were already planted—in his silence, in his hiding, in the nation's refusal to trust God over human power.

Be careful what you wish for. You just might get it.

Turn the page.

4

THE KING WHO COULDN'T WAIT

In *Star Wars: Revenge of the Sith*, Anakin Skywalker has everything going for him. He's the most gifted Jedi of his generation. He's respected by the Council. He has a mentor who believes in him and a wife who loves him. The prophecy says he's the Chosen One—destined to bring balance to the Force.

And then he throws it all away.

It doesn't happen in one dramatic moment. It's a series of choices—small compromises, impatient decisions, moments where he trusts his own judgment instead of listening to those who know better. He's afraid of losing Padmé, so he makes a deal with the dark side. He's frustrated with the Jedi Council, so he stops following their guidance. He convinces himself that the rules don't apply to him, that his situation is special, that the ends justify the means.

By the time he realizes what he's done, it's too late. Anakin Skywalker is gone, and Darth Vader has taken his place.

The story of Saul in 1 Samuel 13–15 follows a heartbreakingly similar pattern. Saul started with so much promise—anointed by God, empowered by the Spirit, victorious in battle.

But through a series of impatient, self-justified decisions, he lost everything. Not his life (that would come later), but something worse: his kingdom, his calling, and his relationship with God.

These chapters show us how a chosen king became a rejected one. And they warn us that the path from promise to ruin is often paved with excuses that sound perfectly reasonable.

THE FIRST FAILURE

Things started well enough. Saul had assembled an army. His son Jonathan—who would prove to be far braver than his father—had just struck down a Philistine outpost at Geba. It was a bold move that got the enemy's attention. The Philistines gathered a massive army in response: thousands of chariots, thousands of horsemen, and foot soldiers "as numerous as the sand on the seashore."

When the Israelites saw what they were up against, they panicked. Soldiers hid in caves, among rocks, in pits and cisterns. Some deserted entirely, crossing the Jordan River to get as far away as possible. Saul's army was melting away like snow in the sun.

Saul was at Gilgal, waiting for Samuel. Back when Samuel had first anointed Saul, he had given him specific instructions: "Go down to Gilgal ahead of me. I will surely come down to you to offer burnt offerings and sacrifice peace offerings. Wait seven days until I come to you, and I will show you what you are to do."

This was important. Samuel was the prophet—the one who spoke for God. He would come, offer the sacrifices, and give Saul divine direction for the battle. Saul's job was to wait.

So Saul waited. Day one. Day two. Day three. The army kept shrinking. Day four. Day five. Day six. The Philistines were getting closer. Day seven arrived, and still no Samuel. The remaining soldiers were "quaking with fear." More were deserting every hour.

Saul couldn't take it anymore. "Bring me the burnt offering and the peace offerings," he said. And Saul offered the sacrifice himself. Just as he finished, Samuel arrived.

"WHAT HAVE YOU DONE?"

Samuel's first words were a question that echoes through Scripture whenever God's people make terrible choices: "What have you done?"

Saul had his explanation ready. It was a good explanation, actually—logical, reasonable, and full of legitimate concerns: "When I saw that the men were scattering from me, and that you did not come within the days appointed, and that the Philistines had assembled at Michmash, I thought, 'Now the Philistines will come down against me at Gilgal, and I have not sought the favor of the LORD.' So I forced myself, and offered the burnt offering."

Did you catch all the excuses? The soldiers were leaving. Samuel was late. The enemy was advancing. Saul needed God's blessing before battle. What else was he supposed to do? He "forced himself"—he didn't want to do it, but circumstances left him no choice!

It all sounded so reasonable. But Samuel wasn't buying it. "You have done foolishly," the prophet said. "You have not kept the command of the LORD your God, which he commanded you. For then the LORD would have established your kingdom over Israel forever. But now your kingdom shall not continue. The LORD has sought out a man after his own heart, and the LORD has commanded him to be prince over his people, because you have not kept what the LORD commanded you."

The verdict was devastating. Saul's dynasty was finished before it really began. His sons would not inherit the throne. God had already chosen someone else—"a man after his own heart"—to replace him.

And all because Saul couldn't wait.

WAS THE PUNISHMENT TOO HARSH?

This is where a lot of readers get stuck. Was what Saul did really that bad? He offered a sacrifice—isn't that a good thing? The situation was desperate. Samuel was late. Soldiers were deserting. Couldn't God cut Saul some slack?

But here's what we need to understand: Saul's sin wasn't about the sacrifice itself. It was about what the sacrifice revealed—a heart that valued its own judgment over God's word.

God had given clear instructions through Samuel: wait for me. Don't act until I tell you what to do. Saul's job wasn't to figure things out on his own; it was to trust and obey.

Instead, Saul decided that the emergency changed the rules. He decided that his assessment of the situation was more reliable than God's command. He decided that he could proceed without prophetic direction because—surely—God would understand.

But that's exactly the problem. Saul was supposed to be a different kind of king—one who ruled under God's authority, not independently of it. If the king could set aside God's word whenever circumstances seemed to justify it, then Israel was no different from all the other nations. The whole point of having a covenant king was that he would lead the people in following God, not in doing whatever seemed right in the moment.

Saul failed the test. And the test wasn't whether he could win battles—it was whether he would trust God's word even when it was hard.

ONE MORE CHANCE

You might think that after such a severe rebuke, Saul would be extra careful to obey God's commands. But that's not what happened.

Some time later, Samuel came to Saul with a new assignment from God: "I will punish the Amalekites for what they did to Israel when they waylaid them as they came up from Egypt. Now go, attack the Amalekites and totally destroy all that belongs to them. Do not spare them; put to death men and women, children and infants, cattle and sheep, camels and donkeys."

This sounds brutal to modern ears, and we need to acknowledge that. The Amalekites had been enemies of God's people since the exodus, attacking Israel when they were weak and vulnerable. This judgment had been announced centuries earlier. It wasn't genocide for land or resources—it was divine judgment on a nation that had set itself against God's purposes.

The key word was "totally destroy." In ancient warfare, this meant everything—no plunder, no prisoners, no livestock kept as spoils of war. Everything was to be devoted to the Lord as an act of judgment and worship.

Saul went to battle and won a decisive victory. But then he made a choice that would seal his fate. "Saul and the army spared Agag"—the Amalekite king—"and the best of the sheep and cattle, the fat calves and lambs—everything that was good. These they were unwilling to destroy completely, but everything that was despised and weak they totally destroyed."

Saul obeyed the parts of God's command that were easy. He destroyed everything worthless. But when it came to the valuable stuff—the prize livestock, the captured king who could be paraded as a trophy—he decided God's instructions needed some adjustment.

"I HAVE CARRIED OUT THE LORD'S INSTRUCTIONS"

God spoke to Samuel that night: "I regret that I have made Saul king, because he has turned away from me and has not carried out my instructions."

Samuel was so upset he cried out to the Lord all night long. The next morning, he went to find Saul. Saul greeted him cheerfully: "The LORD bless you! I have carried out the LORD's instructions."

The audacity of that statement is breathtaking. Saul stood there, surrounded by the bleating sheep and lowing cattle he had spared, and claimed to have fully obeyed God. He had convinced himself that partial obedience was the same as complete obedience.

Samuel's response is one of the most famous lines in the Old Testament: "What then is this bleating of sheep in my ears? What is this lowing of cattle that I hear?"

Busted.

Saul immediately started making excuses. "The soldiers brought them from the Amalekites; they spared the best of the sheep and cattle to sacrifice to the LORD your God, but we totally destroyed the rest."

Notice what he did there? First, he blamed the soldiers—it wasn't his decision; it was theirs. Second, he claimed a pious motive—they were going to sacrifice the animals to God! Surely that makes it okay, right?

Samuel had heard enough. "Stop! Let me tell you what the LORD said to me last night."

TO OBEY IS BETTER THAN SACRIFICE

What followed is one of the most important statements about God and worship in the entire Bible: "Does the LORD delight in burnt offerings and sacrifices as much as in obeying the LORD? To obey is better than sacrifice, and to heed is better than the fat of rams. For rebellion is like the sin of divination, and arrogance like the evil of idolatry. Because you have rejected the word of the LORD, he has rejected you as king."

Read that again slowly.

Saul thought he could substitute religious activity for actual obedience. He thought that if he sacrificed some of the animals to God, that would cover his disobedience in keeping them in the first place. He was treating worship like a transaction—like he could pay off his sin with burnt offerings.

But God doesn't want our sacrifices if our hearts aren't submitted to him. He doesn't want worship from people who ignore his commands. He's not interested in religious rituals performed by rebels.

Samuel compared Saul's rebellion to divination—the pagan practice of trying to manipulate spiritual forces. He compared his arrogance to idolatry—the worship of false gods. Why? Because when we decide we know better than God, we're essentially setting ourselves up as our own god. We're worshiping our own judgment instead of submitting to his.

Then came the devastating wordplay: "Because you have rejected the word of the LORD, he has rejected you as king." Saul rejected God's word. So God rejected Saul.

REPENTANCE THAT WASN'T

Now Saul admitted his sin: "I have sinned. I violated the LORD's command and your instructions. I was afraid of the men and so I gave in to them. Now I beg you, forgive my sin and come back with me, so that I may worship the LORD."

Finally! Confession! This sounds like repentance, right? But Samuel wasn't convinced. He turned to leave. Saul grabbed the hem of his robe, and it tore.

Samuel used the moment as a parable: "The LORD has torn the kingdom of Israel from you today and has given it to one of your neighbors—to one better than you. He who is the Glory of Israel does not lie or change his mind; for he is not a human being, that he should change his mind."

Saul tried again: "I have sinned. But please honor me before the elders of my people and before Israel; come back with me, so that I may worship the LORD your God."

And there it was—the tell. "Please honor me before the elders." Saul's concern wasn't reconciliation with God. It was his reputation with people. He wanted Samuel to come back so that publicly, everything would look fine. He cared more about appearing honorable than about actually being restored.

That's the difference between true repentance and fake repentance. True repentance cares about the relationship with God. Fake repentance cares about managing the consequences.

Samuel did return with Saul—not to honor him, but to finish the job Saul had failed to do. The old prophet called for Agag, the Amalekite king, and executed him personally. Then Samuel went home to Ramah.

He never saw Saul again.

WHAT THIS MEANS FOR US

So what do we learn from Saul's example in these stories?

First, partial obedience is disobedience. Saul destroyed the worthless stuff but kept what he valued. He obeyed the parts of God's command that were easy or convenient. We do the same thing when we follow God in the areas that cost us nothing but ignore him where it hurts.

Second, circumstances don't override commands. Saul had plenty of reasons why he couldn't wait for Samuel, why he had to keep the best livestock. They all sounded reasonable. But emergencies don't change what God has said. Difficult situations don't give us permission to disobey.

Third, religious activity can't substitute for obedience. Going to church, giving money, serving in ministry—none of these things impress God if we're ignoring his word in other areas of our lives. He wants our hearts submitted to him, not religious performances that cover up rebellion.

Fourth, true repentance cares about God, not just consequences. Saul said all the right words—"I have sinned"—but his real concern was his reputation. When we confess sin, we need to ask ourselves: Am I genuinely grieved that I've offended God, or am I just upset about getting caught?

Fifth, choices have permanent consequences. Saul's dynasty ended before it began. Some opportunities, once lost, don't come back. The grace of God is endless, but that doesn't mean every consequence can be reversed. What we do matters.

TALKING POINTS

1. **Saul had reasonable-sounding explanations for both his failures.** Why do you think excuses are so dangerous? How can we tell the difference between a legitimate reason and a self-serving excuse?

2. **Samuel said that "to obey is better than sacrifice."** What are some ways people today try to substitute religious activities for actual obedience to God?

3. **When Saul confessed his sin, he seemed more concerned about his reputation than his relationship with God.** How can you tell if your repentance is genuine or just damage control?

4. **God said he had found "a man after his own heart" to replace Saul.** What do you think that phrase means? What would it look like for someone your age to be "after God's heart"?

5. **Saul's failures were a series of small compromises that led to total rejection.** What small compromises do you see people making that could lead to bigger problems later?

Saul started as the chosen one. He ended as the rejected one. Not because he committed one spectacular sin, but because he consistently valued his own judgment over God's word.

The contrast with David—"a man after God's own heart"—will become clearer as the story continues. David wasn't perfect either. He would sin spectacularly. But when confronted, his response would be completely different from Saul's.

The difference between a Saul and a David isn't perfection. It's what you do when you're caught. One makes excuses. The other breaks. Only one of those responses leads to restoration.

Turn the page.

5

THE SHEPHERD AND THE GIANT

In *Harry Potter and the Sorcerer's Stone*, Harry arrives at Hogwarts as a complete nobody. He's an orphan who grew up sleeping in a cupboard under the stairs. He owns nothing but hand-me-downs and broken glasses. He doesn't know the first thing about magic, and he's surrounded by kids from famous wizarding families who've been preparing for this their whole lives.

But there's something about Harry that nobody can see just by looking at him. There's a destiny written on him—literally, in the form of that lightning bolt scar. The greatest wizard in the world, Albus Dumbledore, sees it. He knows that this unremarkable-looking boy with the messy hair is going to change everything.

Meanwhile, everyone else is busy being impressed by the wrong people. Draco Malfoy struts around talking about his family's importance. People whisper about students from ancient magical bloodlines. The school is full of kids who look the part.

But looks can be deceiving. And in the end, it's the kid from the cupboard under the stairs who faces the Dark Lord.

The story of David's anointing and his battle with Goliath follows the same pattern. Everyone is looking at the wrong things—height, strength, experience, impressive armor. But God is looking at something else entirely. And when the dust settles in the Valley of Elah, the whole world learns that the real question isn't "How big is your giant?" but "How big is your God?"

THE SECRET ANOINTING

Samuel was depressed. Ever since God had rejected Saul, the old prophet had been mourning—grieving over what might have been, worrying about what would happen to Israel now that its first king had failed so spectacularly.

God interrupted his grief with a question and a command: "How long will you mourn for Saul, since I have rejected him as king over Israel? Fill your horn with oil and go. I am sending you to Jesse of Bethlehem. I have chosen one of his sons to be king."

Just like that, God was moving forward. He wasn't stuck in the past. He had already provided a replacement—a new king, a man after his own heart. Samuel's job was to stop mourning and start anointing.

But Samuel had a problem. "How can I go?" he asked. "If Saul hears about it, he'll kill me."

This was a legitimate concern. Saul was paranoid and unstable. If he heard that Samuel was anointing a new king, he would view it as treason. Samuel's life would be in danger.

God gave him a cover story: "Take a heifer with you and say, 'I have come to sacrifice to the LORD.' Invite Jesse to the sacrifice, and I will show you what to do."

So Samuel traveled to Bethlehem. When he arrived, the town elders were terrified. "Do you come in peace?" they asked nervously. Samuel's reputation preceded him—this was the man who had publicly confronted King Saul. His unexpected arrival could mean trouble.

"Yes, in peace," Samuel assured them. "I've come to sacrifice to the LORD. Consecrate yourselves and come with me."

He specifically consecrated Jesse and his sons and invited them to the sacrifice. The real business was about to begin.

THE PARADE OF BROTHERS

When Jesse's sons arrived, Samuel saw Eliab and immediately thought, "Surely the LORD's anointed stands here before the LORD." Eliab was impressive. Tall, probably good-looking, with the kind of presence that makes people take notice. Samuel's fingers reached for his horn of oil. This had to be the one.

But God stopped him: "Do not consider his appearance or his height, for I have rejected him. The LORD does not look at the things people look at. People look at the outward appearance, but the LORD looks on the heart."

This is one of the most important verses in the entire book of Samuel. It explains why Saul failed and why David will succeed. It reveals how God operates, and it warns us against trusting our own first impressions.

Samuel had been fooled by appearances before. Remember how Saul was introduced? "An impressive young man without equal among the Israelites—a head taller than anyone else." Israel had wanted a king who looked like a king, and they got one. It didn't work out so well.

Now Samuel was about to make the same mistake. He saw Eliab and thought "king material." God saw Eliab's heart and said "rejected."

Jesse called his next son, Abinadab. Samuel waited for God's signal. "The LORD has not chosen this one either." Then Shammah. "Nor has the LORD chosen this one." One by one, seven of Jesse's sons paraded before Samuel. One by one, God said no.

Finally, Samuel asked the obvious question: "Are these all the sons you have?" Jesse hesitated. "There is still the youngest, but he is out tending the sheep."

The youngest. So insignificant that his own father hadn't bothered to bring him to a sacrifice where a famous prophet was examining the family. So unimportant that he was left in the fields while his brothers got dressed up for the ceremony.

"Send for him," Samuel said. "We will not sit down until he arrives."

THE UNLIKELY KING

They sent for the boy and brought him in. The text describes him as "ruddy"—healthy-looking, with a reddish complexion—"with a fine appearance and handsome features." He was good-looking, but that wasn't why God chose him. Eliab was probably good-looking too.

Then the Lord said to Samuel, "Rise and anoint him; this is the one." Samuel took his horn of oil and anointed David right there in the presence of his brothers. None of them fully understood what was happening. They saw oil poured on their youngest brother's head. They didn't know they were witnessing the beginning of a dynasty that would change the world.

"And from that day on the Spirit of the LORD came powerfully upon David." That's the key detail. David wasn't chosen because he was the best-looking or the strongest or the most experienced. He was chosen because God looked at his heart and saw something there—a heart that was oriented toward God, a heart that God could work with. And when Samuel anointed him, the Spirit of God rushed upon David to equip him for everything that lay ahead.

Meanwhile, the Spirit of the Lord had departed from Saul. In its place, "a harmful spirit from the LORD tormented him." Saul became plagued with dark moods, paranoia, and instability. His servants suggested finding a skilled musician who could play soothing music when the bad spells came.

Someone mentioned a son of Jesse from Bethlehem—"skillful in playing, a man of valor, a man of war, prudent in speech, and a man of good presence, and the LORD is with him."

So Saul sent for David. And David, the secretly anointed future king, entered the court of the current king as a servant. He became Saul's armor-bearer. He played his harp when the harmful spirit tormented Saul. And Saul loved him—at least for now. It was the beginning of a complicated relationship that would define both of their lives.

THE GIANT'S CHALLENGE

Some time later, the Philistines gathered their armies for war. They camped on one hill; the Israelites camped on another, with the Valley of Elah between them.

Then a champion came out from the Philistine camp. His name was Goliath, from the city of Gath.

The description of Goliath is meant to terrify you. He was over nine feet tall. He wore a bronze helmet and a coat of armor weighing 125 pounds. He had bronze armor on his legs and a bronze javelin slung on his back. His spear shaft was "like a weaver's beam," and its iron point weighed fifteen pounds. He had a shield-bearer who walked ahead of him.

This was a walking tank. A monster. A one-man army.

And every day, morning and evening for forty days, Goliath walked out into the valley and shouted his challenge: "Why do you come out and line up for battle? Am I not a Philistine, and are you not the servants of Saul? Choose a man and have him come down to me. If he is able to fight and kill me, we will become your subjects; but if I overcome him and kill him, you will become our subjects and serve us. This day I defy the armies of Israel! Give me a man and let us fight each other!"

When Saul and all the Israelites heard this, they were "dismayed and terrified." No one volunteered. No one was willing to face the giant. Day after day, Goliath strutted into the valley and mocked the armies of Israel, and day after day, Israel did nothing.

THE ERRAND BOY

David wasn't at the battle. He had gone back home to tend his father's sheep in Bethlehem. But his three oldest brothers were with Saul's army.

One day Jesse sent David to the front lines with supplies—roasted grain, bread, and cheese for the commander. "See how your brothers are doing," Jesse said. "Bring back some assurance from them."

David arrived at the camp just as the army was going out to its battle positions, shouting the war cry. He left his supplies with the keeper of the baggage and ran to the battle lines to greet his brothers.

That's when Goliath appeared for his daily challenge.

David watched the Israelite soldiers flee in terror. He listened as men around him talked about what Saul had promised to whoever killed the giant: great wealth, the king's daughter in marriage, and tax exemption for the man's family.

David started asking questions. "What will be done for the man who kills this Philistine and removes this disgrace from Israel? Who is this uncircumcised Philistine that he should defy the armies of the living God?"

Did you catch what David called Goliath? "This uncircumcised Philistine." In other words: this pagan outsider who doesn't know the God of Israel. David didn't see a nine-foot monster. He saw a man who was defying the living God—and that offended him.

David's oldest brother Eliab heard him talking and got angry. "Why have you come down here? And with whom did you leave those few sheep in the wilderness? I know how conceited you are and how wicked your heart is; you came down only to watch the battle."

Classic big brother. Dismissive, insulting, assuming the worst. But David didn't take the bait. "Now what have I done? Can't I even speak?" He turned away and kept asking questions.

Word reached Saul that some young man was asking about the giant. Saul sent for David.

"I'LL FIGHT HIM"

Standing before the king, David said something nobody expected: "Let no one lose heart on account of this Philistine; your servant will go and fight him."

Saul's response was reasonable: "You are not able to go out against this Philistine and fight him; you are only a young man, and he has been a warrior from his youth."

But David had an answer. "Your servant has been keeping his father's sheep. When a lion or a bear came and carried off a sheep from the flock, I went after it, struck it and rescued the sheep from its mouth. When it turned on me, I seized it by its hair, struck it and killed it. Your servant has killed both the lion and the bear; this uncircumcised Philistine will be like one of them, because he has defied the armies of the living God. The LORD who rescued me from the paw of the lion and the paw of the bear will rescue me from the hand of this Philistine."

This is important. David wasn't being reckless or overconfident. He had experience—not with human armies, but with deadly predators in the wilderness. More importantly, he had experience with God's deliverance. He had seen God save him from the lion. He had seen God save him from the bear. He was confident God would save him from the giant.

David's faith wasn't blind faith. It was built on a track record of God's faithfulness.

Saul finally agreed. "Go, and the LORD be with you." Then Saul dressed David in his own armor—a coat of armor, a bronze helmet, a sword. David tried walking around in it and quickly realized it wouldn't work. "I cannot go in these," he said, "because I am not used to them." He took off the armor.

David picked up his shepherd's staff and chose five smooth stones from the stream. He put them in the pouch of his shepherd's bag. With his sling in his hand, he approached the Philistine.

THE BATTLE

Goliath looked at David and was insulted. "Am I a dog, that you come at me with sticks?" He cursed David by his gods. "Come here, and I'll give your flesh to the birds and the wild animals!"

David's response is one of the greatest speeches in the Bible: "You come against me with sword and spear and javelin, but I come against you in the name of the LORD Almighty, the God of the armies of Israel, whom you have defied. This day the LORD will deliver you into my hands, and I'll strike you down and cut off your head. This very day I will give the carcasses of the Philistine army to the birds and the wild animals, and the whole world will know that there is a God in Israel. All those gathered here will know that it is not by sword or spear that the LORD saves; for the battle is the LORD's, and he will give all of you into our hands."

Notice what David emphasized. Not his own skill. Not his own bravery. The battle belongs to the LORD. The LORD will deliver. The whole world will know there is a God in Israel. David was fighting for God's honor, not his own.

Goliath moved forward. David ran—not away, but toward the giant. He reached into his bag, took out a stone, slung it, and struck Goliath on the forehead. The stone sank in. Goliath fell face-down on the ground. David ran and stood over him.

He took Goliath's own sword, drew it from the sheath, and cut off his head.

When the Philistines saw that their champion was dead, they turned and ran. The Israelite army surged forward with a shout, chasing the Philistines all the way to the gates of their cities. Then they returned and plundered the Philistine camp.

David took Goliath's head to Jerusalem and kept his weapons as trophies.

WHAT THIS MEANS FOR US

First, God sees what we can't see. Samuel looked at Eliab and saw a king. God looked at David and saw a heart. We judge by appearances—height, strength, popularity, credentials. God judges by what's inside. That's good news for everyone who feels overlooked.

Second, faithfulness in small things prepares us for big things. David wasn't trained in a military academy. He learned courage and skill protecting sheep from lions and bears. His lonely, unglamorous job in the wilderness prepared him for his moment in the spotlight. Never despise the small assignments.

Third, the right question changes everything. Everyone else asked, "How can we possibly beat this giant?" David asked, "Who is this pagan that he should defy the living God?" Same situation, completely different perspective. When you face your giants, ask the right questions.

Fourth, faith is built on experience. David wasn't guessing that God would help him. He had seen God deliver him before. Your history with God—even in small things—becomes the foundation for trusting him in bigger things.

Fifth, the battle belongs to the Lord. David won not because he was stronger or better equipped than Goliath—he obviously wasn't. He won because God fought for him. When you're on God's side, fighting for God's honor, you have resources the world can't see.

TALKING POINTS

Here are some questions to consider and discuss:

1. **God told Samuel, "People look at the outward appearance, but the LORD looks on the heart."** What are some ways we judge people by their outward appearance? How might God see those same people differently?

2. **David's experience fighting lions and bears prepared him to fight Goliath.** What "small" challenges in your life right now might be preparing you for something bigger later?

3. **Everyone in Israel was terrified of Goliath.** David was offended by him. What made David see the situation so differently?

4. **David refused to wear Saul's armor because "I am not used to them."** What's the lesson there? Why is it important to be yourself instead of trying to be someone else?

5. **David said, "The battle is the LORD's."** What does that mean for how we face our own "giants"—big problems or scary situations that seem impossible to overcome?

A shepherd boy with a sling. A giant with a spear. By every human calculation, the outcome should have been obvious.

But God doesn't calculate the way humans do. He doesn't look at the size of the warrior; he looks at the size of the faith. He doesn't count the weapons; he counts the hearts that trust him.

David walked into that valley with nothing but five stones and a God who keeps his promises. It was more than enough.

Turn the page.

6

THE BEST FRIEND AND THE JEALOUS KING

In *The Lord of the Rings*, Samwise Gamgee makes a promise to Gandalf: "Don't you leave him, Samwise Gamgee." And Sam doesn't. Through Mordor's wasteland, up the slopes of Mount Doom, when Frodo can barely walk and the Ring is destroying him from the inside out, Sam stays. He carries Frodo on his back when Frodo can't carry himself. He fights off giant spiders and orcs. He nearly starves.

Why? Because Sam made a promise. Because Frodo is his friend. Because some loyalties go deeper than comfort, deeper than safety, deeper even than survival.

Sam could have gone home. Nobody would have blamed him. The mission was Frodo's, not his. But Sam understood something that most people never grasp: true friendship isn't about what you get out of it. It's about what you're willing to give.

The story of David and Jonathan in 1 Samuel 18-20 is one of the greatest friendship stories ever told. It's also one of the most costly. Jonathan was the crown prince—next in line to be king. David was the shepherd boy God had chosen to take that throne. By every rule of politics and self-preservation, Jonathan should have seen David as his enemy.

Instead, he saw a brother.

And that choice would cost him everything.

SOUL MATES

After David's stunning victory over Goliath, everything changed. He wasn't going back to the sheep. Saul kept him at court, gave him military commands, and treated him like family.

But the most significant thing that happened after the giant fell wasn't David's promotion—it was his friendship with Jonathan. "The soul of Jonathan was knit to the soul of David, and Jonathan loved him as his own soul."

Jonathan was Saul's oldest son—a proven warrior himself, the hero of the battle at Michmash where he had trusted God against impossible odds. He was everything a crown prince should be: brave, capable, respected. By rights, he should have been threatened by this newcomer who was suddenly getting all the attention.

Instead, Jonathan made a covenant with David. He stripped off his own robe—the robe of the crown prince—and gave it to David. He handed over his armor, his sword, his bow, his belt. These weren't just gifts. In that culture, your clothes represented who you were. By giving David his royal garments, Jonathan was symbolically saying, "I know the kingdom is supposed to be yours, not mine. And I'm okay with that."

Think about how crazy that is. Jonathan was giving away his future. He was renouncing his claim to the throne. He was looking at the guy who would replace his family dynasty and saying, "I choose friendship with you over power for myself."

Nobody did that in the ancient world. When a new dynasty threatened your family's rule, you didn't befriend the rival—you eliminated him. That was just how things worked.

But Jonathan wasn't playing by the world's rules. He was playing by God's.

THE SONG THAT CHANGED EVERYTHING

David kept succeeding at everything Saul assigned him. He led military campaigns and won them. He was promoted to command over the fighting men. The Bible repeats the same phrase over and over: "The LORD was with him." That was the secret of David's success—not his skill or charm, but God's presence.

Everyone loved David. The soldiers respected him. The servants admired him. Even Saul's own children were drawn to him—Jonathan as his best friend, and eventually Michal, Saul's daughter, fell in love with him too. But something was building in Saul's heart. Something dark.

When the army returned from defeating the Philistines, women came out from all the towns of Israel, dancing and singing, celebrating the victory. And they sang this song: "Saul has struck down his thousands, and David his ten thousands."

It was just a victory chant. The women weren't trying to make a political statement. In Hebrew poetry, you often repeated ideas with bigger numbers the second time—it was a style thing, not a math thing. They were celebrating both Saul and David.

But Saul didn't hear it that way. "They have credited David with ten thousands," he fumed, "but me with only thousands. What more can he have but the kingdom?"

From that day on, Saul watched David with suspicion. The text says he "eyed" David—kept him under surveillance, looking for any excuse to take him down. The man who had once loved David now feared him. And fear, in Saul's twisted heart, quickly turned to hatred.

SPEARS AND SCHEMES

The very next day, while David was playing his harp to soothe Saul's troubled spirit—the same job he'd been doing since he first came to court—Saul had a spear in his hand. Suddenly, without warning, he hurled it at David, trying to pin him to the wall.

David dodged. Twice.

Now, you might think David would have figured out at this point that Saul wanted him dead. But the text suggests David didn't fully grasp what was happening. Saul's "spells" were well known at court. When the harmful spirit came upon him, Saul acted erratically. David probably thought this was just another episode of Saul's madness—dangerous, but not deliberately murderous.

He was wrong. But he didn't know it yet.

Saul removed David from his personal staff and put him in command of a thousand soldiers. This sounds like a promotion, but it was actually a scheme. If David was constantly out fighting Philistines, eventually he'd get killed. Saul could let the enemy do his dirty work.

But it didn't work. "In everything he did David had great success, because the LORD was with him."

Saul became even more afraid.

Then Saul tried another approach. He offered David his older daughter Merab as a wife—but with a catch. David would have to keep fighting the LORD's battles. What Saul really meant was: keep fighting until you die. But at the last minute, Saul broke his promise and gave Merab to someone else.

When Saul learned that his younger daughter Michal loved David, he got another idea. He sent servants to David with an offer: "The king wants no bride-price except a hundred Philistine foreskins."

This was a death sentence disguised as a wedding present. To collect that grim trophy, David would have to kill a hundred Philistine warriors in close combat. Surely he'd be killed in the attempt.

David went out and killed two hundred Philistines. He brought back the proof. He married Michal.

Saul's fear grew into full-blown terror. "When Saul realized that the LORD was with David and that his daughter Michal loved him, Saul became still more afraid of him, and he remained his enemy the rest of his days."

The king was now openly at war with his own son-in-law.

JONATHAN'S IMPOSSIBLE POSITION

In chapter 19, things escalated. Saul stopped hiding his intentions. He told Jonathan and all his attendants directly: kill David.

This put Jonathan in an impossible position. His father was the king—his commander, his family, his duty. But David was his covenant brother—bound by sacred oath, the deepest friendship of his life. What do you do when the two most important loyalties in your life come into direct conflict?

Jonathan chose David.

He warned David to hide. Then he went to his father and pleaded David's case: "Let not the king sin against his servant David, because he has not sinned against you, and because his deeds have brought good to you. He took his life in his hand and struck down the Philistine, and the LORD worked a great salvation for all Israel. You saw it and rejoiced. Why then will you sin against innocent blood by killing David without cause?"

Saul listened. He even swore an oath: "As the LORD lives, he shall not be put to death." Jonathan brought David back. For a while, things seemed okay.

But it didn't last. David won another battle against the Philistines, and when he returned, Saul's dark moods returned with him. Again David was playing his harp. Again Saul had a spear. Again the spear flew at David's head—and again David escaped.

This time, David ran home. But Saul sent men to watch the house and kill David in the morning. Michal—Saul's own daughter—helped David escape through a window, then put a household idol in his bed with goat hair on its head to fool the soldiers.

When Saul found out, he was furious. "Why did you deceive me and let my enemy escape?" His own daughter had chosen David over him.

THE ARROW SIGNAL

David was now a fugitive. He ran to Samuel at Ramah, but Saul tracked him there. He ran back to find Jonathan, desperate to understand what was happening.

"What have I done?" David asked. "What is my crime? What sin have I committed against your father that he's trying to kill me?"

Jonathan couldn't believe it had gotten this bad. "Never! You're not going to die. My father doesn't do anything without telling me. Why would he hide this from me?"

But David knew better. "Your father knows very well that I have found favor in your eyes, and he's thinking, 'Jonathan must not know this or he will be grieved.' But as surely as the LORD lives and as you live, there is only a step between me and death."

Jonathan believed him. Together, they came up with a plan. The next day was the new moon festival—a monthly celebration where David would normally eat at the king's table. David would hide in a field. Jonathan would attend the feast and observe Saul's reaction when David's seat was empty. If Saul was calm about David's absence, things might be okay. If he exploded, David would know for certain: run and never come back.

They agreed on a signal. Jonathan would come to the field the next day with a young boy to collect arrows. If Jonathan shot the arrows short and told the boy, "The arrows are on this side of you," it meant David was safe. If he shot them beyond the boy and called out, "The arrows are beyond you," it meant David had to flee.

Before they parted, Jonathan made David renew their covenant—not just for themselves, but for their descendants. "May the LORD be between me and you, and between my offspring and your offspring, forever."

Jonathan knew what was coming. He was preparing for a future where they might never see each other again.

THE BREAKING POINT

David hid in the field. The new moon feast began. Saul sat in his usual place, against the wall—the safest seat, the king's seat. Jonathan sat across from him. Abner, the army commander, sat beside Saul. David's place was empty.

The first day, Saul said nothing. He assumed David must be ceremonially unclean—unable to participate in a sacred meal. No big deal. He'd be there tomorrow.

The second day, David's seat was still empty. Saul asked Jonathan, "Why hasn't the son of Jesse come to the meal, either yesterday or today?"

Notice what Saul called David: "the son of Jesse." Not David. Not "your friend." Just a dismissive reference to his father. Saul was already distancing himself, already treating David as an enemy.

Jonathan delivered the cover story they'd prepared: David had asked permission to attend a family sacrifice in Bethlehem. Saul exploded. "You son of a perverse, rebellious woman! Don't I know that you have sided with the son of Jesse to your own shame? As long as the son of Jesse lives on this earth, neither you nor your kingdom will be established. Now send someone to bring him to me, for he must die!"

Jonathan tried to reason with him. "Why should he be put to death? What has he done?"

Saul's answer was a spear. He hurled it at his own son—the crown prince, his firstborn, his heir—trying to kill him.

Jonathan left the table in fierce anger. He didn't eat anything the rest of the day. He was grieved—not for himself, but for David, because of "his father's shameful treatment of David."

THE FAREWELL

The next morning, Jonathan went to the field with a young boy. He shot an arrow beyond the boy and called out the signal: "Isn't the arrow beyond you? Hurry! Go quickly! Don't stop!" The boy had no idea what was really happening. He collected the arrows and brought them back. Jonathan sent him home with the equipment.

Then David came out of hiding. He fell on his face before Jonathan and bowed three times. They kissed each other—a gesture of friendship and farewell. They wept together—but David wept the most.

Jonathan spoke the last words: "Go in peace, for we have sworn friendship with each other in the name of the LORD, saying, 'The LORD is witness between you and me, and between your descendants and my descendants forever.'" Then David rose and left. And Jonathan went back into the city.

One sentence. Two friends. Two different directions. The fugitive heading into the wilderness. The prince returning to his father's broken kingdom. They would see each other only once more before Jonathan's death.

WHAT THIS MEANS FOR US

First, true friendship costs something. Jonathan gave up his claim to the throne for David. He risked his father's fury. He nearly died for his friend. Cheap friendship isn't friendship at all—it's just mutual convenience.

Second, jealousy destroys from the inside out. Saul had everything—a kingdom, a family, military victories. But jealousy over David's success poisoned all of it. He ended up trying to murder his own son. That's what unchecked envy does: it makes you destroy the very things you should treasure.

Third, loyalty to God sometimes costs us other relationships. Jonathan had to choose between his father and his friend—between family loyalty and faithfulness to God's purposes. Following God doesn't always make family relationships easier. Sometimes it makes them harder.

Fourth, covenant faithfulness provides peace in chaos. Jonathan told David, "Go in peace." That sounds strange when David was about to become a hunted fugitive. But the peace wasn't about circumstances—it was about their relationship. Whatever else happened, their friendship was secure.

Fifth, some people will recognize God's work in your life—and hate you for it. David's success came from God. Saul knew it. And instead of submitting to what God was doing, Saul fought against it. Some opposition comes precisely because God is with you.

TALKING POINTS

Here are a few items to think about and talk through:

1. **Jonathan gave David his royal robe and weapons.** What do you think that cost him emotionally? Why do you think he did it?

2. **Saul heard the women's song and immediately as-**

sumed the worst. How does jealousy distort the way we hear and see things?

3. **Jonathan was caught between his father and his friend.** Have you ever been caught between two loyalties? How did you handle it?

4. **When Saul threw a spear at Jonathan, it revealed how far his hatred of David had corrupted him.** What does this teach us about letting anger and fear go unchecked?

5. **Jonathan told David to "go in peace" even though David was about to become a fugitive.** What kind of peace was he talking about? How is that different from our usual idea of peace?

David walked away from that field with nothing but the clothes on his back and a covenant promise in his heart. He had lost his position, his home, his wife, his safety. But he hadn't lost his friend. And he hadn't lost his God. Sometimes that's all you have. Sometimes that's enough.

Turn the page.

7

ON THE RUN

In Robert Louis Stevenson's classic novel *Kidnapped*, young David Balfour thinks he's going to claim his inheritance. Instead, his wicked uncle has him knocked on the head and thrown onto a ship headed for the American colonies to be sold as a slave. David escapes when the ship wrecks off the coast of Scotland—but now he's stranded in the wild Highlands with no money, no friends, and powerful people who want him dead or gone.

For most of the book, David is on the run. He hides in heather. He sleeps in caves. He nearly starves. He has to trust strangers who might betray him at any moment. Every day is about survival, about making it to the next hiding place, about staying one step ahead of the people hunting him.

That's David's life—the biblical David—for the next several years. After the tearful farewell with Jonathan, David is officially a fugitive. Saul has declared him an enemy of the state. There's no going home, no returning to normal life, no appealing to anyone for help. David is running for his life, and he'll keep running until either he dies or Saul does.

These chapters (1 Samuel 21–23) show us what that running looked like—the desperate decisions, the unlikely allies, the narrow escapes. They also show us something else: even when David was at his lowest and most confused, God never stopped protecting him. Even when David made mistakes (and he made some big ones), God's hand was still guiding his path. Being on the run doesn't mean being alone.

BREAD AND A SWORD

David's first stop was Nob, a small town just north of Jerusalem where a group of priests operated a sanctuary. The head priest, Ahimelech, was surprised and nervous when David showed up alone. This was strange—David was a military commander who normally traveled with soldiers. Why was he by himself?

David told a story. The king had sent him on a secret mission, he said. Very hush-hush. His men would meet him later. He just needed some food and, if possible, a weapon.

Was David lying? Probably—at least partly. He was certainly hiding the truth that he was fleeing from Saul. Some have suggested David was trying to protect Ahimelech by not telling him the full story. If Ahimelech didn't know David was running from the king, he couldn't be accused of knowingly helping a fugitive.

Whatever David's motives, Ahimelech helped him. The only bread available was the "bread of the Presence"—twelve loaves that were placed before God in the sanctuary each week, normally eaten only by the priests. But human need took priority over ceremonial rules. Ahimelech gave David the holy bread to keep him alive.

As for weapons, there was only one available: the sword of Goliath the Philistine. David had apparently dedicated it to the sanctuary after his famous victory. Now he needed it back. "There is none like it," David said. "Give it to me."

But there was a witness to this encounter—someone David didn't notice or didn't think about. Doeg the Edomite, one of Saul's servants, was at the sanctuary that day. He saw everything. He heard everything. And he would remember.

ROCK BOTTOM IN GATH

What David did next makes you question his sanity. He fled to Gath—the hometown of Goliath, the Philistine city whose champion he had killed and decapitated. David walked into enemy territory carrying Goliath's own sword.

What was he thinking? Maybe he hoped the Philistine king, Achish, would welcome a defector from Israel's army. Maybe he thought his reputation as an enemy of Saul would make him useful to the Philistines. Maybe he was just so desperate that enemy territory seemed safer than anywhere in Israel.

It was a terrible miscalculation.

The servants of Achish recognized him immediately. "Isn't this David, the king of the land?" they asked. "Isn't he the one they sing about—'Saul has slain his thousands, and David his ten thousands'?"

David heard their words and was terrified. He realized he had walked into a trap. The Philistines weren't going to welcome him as an ally—they were going to kill him. This was the man who had slaughtered their champion and led Israel to victory after victory against their armies.

So David did something crazy. He pretended to be insane. He scratched marks on the doors of the city gate. He let spit dribble down his beard. He acted like a complete madman.

King Achish was disgusted. "Look at the man! He's insane! Why bring him to me? Am I so short of madmen that you have to bring this fellow here to carry on like this? Must this man come into my house?" They let David go. A crazy man wasn't worth the trouble.

It was humiliating. It was degrading. David, the giant-slayer, the king-in-waiting, was drooling on himself and scratching walls like a lunatic. But it worked. He escaped with his life.

Later, David would write psalms about this experience (Psalm 34 and Psalm 56). Even in his most desperate and degrading moments, he would look back and see God's protection. "I sought the LORD, and he answered me; he delivered me from all my fears."

THE CAVE AND THE MISFITS

David escaped to a cave near a town called Adullam, in the low hills of western Judah. Word spread that he was there, and people started coming to him.

Not the kind of people you'd expect to rally around a future king. "All those who were in distress or in debt or discontented gathered around him, and he became their leader. About four hundred men were with him."

In distress. In debt. Discontented. This was David's army—a ragtag collection of society's rejects and failures. Men who had lost everything. Men who owed money they couldn't pay. Men who were fed up with how things were going in Israel.

Not exactly elite soldiers. But David took them in, organized them, and became their captain.

Meanwhile, David was worried about his parents. They were elderly, and if Saul discovered where they were, he might hurt them to get at David. So David traveled to Moab—the country east of the Dead Sea—and asked its king to give his parents sanctuary.

Why would the king of Moab help David? Possibly because of David's ancestry. His great-grandmother Ruth had been a Moabite woman. That connection might have opened doors. Whatever the reason, the king of Moab agreed to shelter David's parents "until I learn what God will do for me."

That phrase reveals something important about David's mindset. He didn't know what was going to happen next. He didn't have a master plan. He was waiting, watching, trying to figure out what God was doing. He was living one day at a time, trusting that somehow God would work things out.

THE MASSACRE AT NOB

Back in Israel, Saul was growing more paranoid by the day. He sat under a tamarisk tree on a hill, spear in hand, surrounded by his officials. He ranted at them about conspiracy. Everyone was against him. No one told him anything. Even his own son had sided with David.

Then Doeg the Edomite spoke up. He had been at Nob. He had seen David come to Ahimelech the priest. He had watched the priest give David food and the sword of Goliath.

Saul was furious. He summoned Ahimelech and all the priests of Nob to stand before him. "Why have you conspired against me?" he demanded. "You gave him bread and a sword! You inquired of God for him!"

Ahimelech's defense was reasonable and truthful: "Who of all your servants is as loyal as David, the king's son-in-law, captain of your bodyguard, highly respected in your household? I have often inquired of God for him. Why does the king accuse his servant of anything?"

It didn't matter. Saul had already made up his mind. "You will surely die, Ahimelech, you and your whole family." The king ordered his guards to kill the priests. But they refused. These were the Lord's priests. The guards couldn't bring themselves to raise their hands against God's servants.

So Saul turned to Doeg. Doeg had no such scruples. That day, he killed eighty-five priests who wore the linen ephod—the special garment of those who served at the sanctuary. Then he went to Nob itself and put the entire town to the sword: men, women, children, infants, cattle, donkeys, sheep.

Total destruction. An entire community of priests wiped out because they had unknowingly helped a fugitive.

Only one person escaped: Abiathar, one of Ahimelech's sons. He fled to David and told him everything.

David's response reveals his conscience: "I knew it that day, when Doeg the Edomite was there, that he would be sure to tell Saul. I have brought about the death of all the persons of your father's house."

David took responsibility. He hadn't swung the sword, but his deception at Nob had set this tragedy in motion. "Stay with me," he told Abiathar. "Don't be afraid. The man who is seeking your life is seeking mine also. With me you will be safe."

From that point on, Abiathar the priest stayed with David. And because Abiathar had the ephod—the device priests used to inquire of God—David now had a direct way to seek God's guidance. God brought something good out of something terrible.

RESCUE AT KEILAH

David heard that the Philistines were attacking a town called Keilah, robbing the threshing floors where people stored their grain. Saul, the king who was supposed to protect Israel, was too busy hunting David to defend his own people.

But David wasn't too busy. He inquired of the LORD through Abiathar: "Should I go and attack these Philistines?" God answered: "Go, attack the Philistines and save Keilah."

David's men were terrified. "We're afraid just being here in Judah," they said. "How much worse if we go to Keilah against the Philistine forces!"

So David inquired again. And again God answered: "Go down to Keilah, for I am going to give the Philistines into your hand." David trusted the word. He attacked. He won. He saved the town.

But then things got complicated. Saul heard that David was at Keilah—a walled city with gates and bars. "God has delivered him into my hands," Saul gloated. "David has imprisoned himself by entering a town with gates and bars."

Saul began mobilizing his forces to besiege the city. David heard about it. Once again he inquired of the LORD: "Will Saul come down, as your servant has heard? O LORD God of Israel, tell your servant."

"He will come down," God said.

Then David asked the harder question: "Will the citizens of Keilah surrender me and my men to Saul?"

"They will."

David had just saved this town from the Philistines. But if Saul showed up with an army, the people of Keilah would hand David over to save themselves. Gratitude only goes so far when a paranoid king is threatening to destroy your city.

David didn't wait around to test their loyalty. He and his six hundred men left Keilah and kept moving, never staying in one place long enough for Saul to catch them.

JONATHAN'S LAST VISIT

David was hiding in the wilderness of Ziph, moving from place to place, living in the desert strongholds. Saul searched for him every day, but "God did not give David into his hands."

Then Jonathan came to find him. This was dangerous. Jonathan was Saul's son. If anyone was watching, if anyone reported back to Saul, Jonathan could be accused of treason. But he came anyway.

And he did something beautiful: "he helped David find strength in God."

"Don't be afraid," Jonathan said. "My father Saul will not lay a hand on you. You will be king over Israel, and I will be second to you. Even my father Saul knows this."

Think about what Jonathan was saying. He was acknowledging that David would take the throne that should have been his. He was accepting his place as second to his best friend. He was encouraging David with the very promises that meant Jonathan himself would never be king.

They made a covenant together—one more time, one last time—and then Jonathan went home. David never saw him again.

SURROUNDED

The Ziphites—people from David's own tribe of Judah—betrayed him to Saul. They told the king exactly where David was hiding and offered to hand him over.

Saul was delighted. "The LORD bless you for your concern for me," he said. (The irony is thick—Saul invoking the LORD's blessing on people who were betraying the LORD's anointed.)

The chase narrowed. Saul and his men were on one side of a mountain; David and his men were on the other. David was hurrying to get away, but Saul's forces were closing in, surrounding them. It looked like the end.

And then a messenger arrived for Saul: "Come quickly! The Philistines are raiding the land!"

Saul had no choice. He had to abandon the chase and go deal with the invasion. David escaped by the narrowest of margins.

They called that place "the Rock of Escape"—or, more literally, "the Rock of Division," because Saul and David were separated there just when capture seemed certain.

It wasn't luck. It wasn't coincidence. It was God, using the Philistines—Israel's enemies—to save David from Israel's king.

God's timing is perfect. His methods are often surprising.

WHAT THIS MEANS FOR US

First, desperate times can lead to bad decisions—but God's protection doesn't depend on our perfection. David lied to

Ahimelech. He fled to the Philistines. He made choices driven by panic rather than faith. Yet God still protected him. That's grace.

Second, God uses unlikely people and unexpected circumstances. David's army was made up of debtors and malcontents. His escape at the Rock of Division came through a Philistine raid. God isn't limited to working through impressive resources or predictable means.

Third, our choices have consequences for others. David's visit to Nob led to the massacre of the priests. We don't live in isolation. What we do—even when we're just trying to survive—can impact people we never intended to hurt.

Fourth, seeking God's guidance is the key to good decisions. When David inquired of the LORD, he got clear direction. When he acted on his own (like fleeing to Gath), things went badly. The pattern is consistent: ask God first.

Fifth, true friends help us find strength in God. Jonathan didn't just encourage David with nice words. He pointed David to God and to God's promises. That's what real friendship does—it redirects our eyes upward.

TALKING POINTS

Here are some takeaways to consider and discuss:

1. **David pretended to be insane to escape from the Philistines.** Was that wrong, or was it just smart survival? When is it okay to deceive people, if ever?

2. **David's followers were "in distress, in debt, or discontented."** Why do you think these kinds of people were drawn to David? What does it say about David that he accepted them?

3. **The people of Keilah would have handed David over to Saul, even though David had just saved their town.** Why do you think people sometimes betray those who help them?

4. **Jonathan encouraged David by reminding him of God's promises.** Who in your life helps you "find strength in God"? How can you be that person for someone else?

5. **David escaped from Saul because of a Philistine raid—his enemies saved him from his enemy.** What does this teach us about how God works?

David was still running. Still hiding. Still wondering what God was doing. But he wasn't alone. He had his ragtag band of misfits. He had a priest with an ephod. He had the memory of Jonathan's last encouragement. And he had a God who never stopped watching over him—even when the mountain was surrounded and the enemy was closing in.

Sometimes deliverance comes at the last possible moment. But it comes.

Turn the page.

8

THE KING WHO WOULDN'T KILL

In *Spider-Man: No Way Home*, there's a moment when Peter Parker has the chance to kill the Green Goblin. Goblin has caused unimaginable pain—he's responsible for the death of someone Peter loves deeply. Peter has the power. He has the opportunity. Every instinct screams "Do it!"

But Peter doesn't. Even with all that rage and grief, even when revenge seems completely justified, he holds back. He chooses mercy instead of murder.

That choice doesn't make sense to most people. When you have the power to destroy your enemy—especially an enemy who has hurt you over and over—why wouldn't you take the shot?

David faced that exact question. Twice. In 1 Samuel 24 and 26, David has Saul completely at his mercy. The man who has been hunting him like an animal, who has tried to kill him repeatedly, who has murdered innocent priests because of him—that man is suddenly vulnerable. David could end it all with one thrust of a spear.

But he doesn't. And the reason why reveals something profound about what it means to trust God.

THE CAVE AT EN GEDI

After the narrow escape at the Rock of Division, David and his men moved to En Gedi—an oasis on the western shore of the Dead Sea. The area was full of caves, perfect for hiding. Waterfalls cascaded down rocky cliffs. Wild goats scrambled across the crags. It was beautiful and remote.

But Saul wasn't done hunting. As soon as Saul finished dealing with the Philistine raid, he gathered three thousand of his best soldiers and headed for En Gedi. Someone had told him where David was hiding—Saul always seemed to have informants—and he was determined to finish this once and for all.

While searching the area, Saul needed to use the bathroom. He found a cave and went inside for some privacy. He had no idea that David and his men were hiding in the back of that very cave.

Think about the odds of this happening. Thousands of caves in the region, and Saul walks into the one where David is hiding. David's men saw it immediately: this had to be divine providence. God had delivered their enemy into their hands. "This is the day the LORD spoke of," they whispered to David. "He said, 'I will give your enemy into your hands for you to deal with as you wish.'"

David crept forward in the darkness. Saul was completely vulnerable, unaware, defenseless. One strike and it would all be over. No more running. No more fear. No more hiding in caves and deserts. David would be free.

David raised his knife—and cut off a corner of Saul's robe. That's it. Just a piece of fabric. He didn't touch Saul himself. And immediately, David felt terrible about it.

A GUILTY CONSCIENCE

Why would David feel guilty about cutting a piece of cloth? Because of what it meant. In that culture, a king's robe wasn't just clothing—it represented his authority and position. By cutting Saul's robe, David had symbolically attacked Saul's kingship. It was as if he were saying, "I'm taking the kingdom from you." Even that symbolic act felt like too much.

"The LORD forbid that I should do such a thing to my master, the LORD's anointed," David told his men. "I will not lift my hand against him, for he is the LORD's anointed."

David's men were furious. They had Saul right there! They could end this nightmare today! But David "rebuked his men" sharply and would not allow them to attack Saul. His words must have been forceful, because these were battle-hardened warriors who desperately wanted to kill the man hunting them.

Meanwhile, Saul finished his business and walked out of the cave, completely unaware of how close he had come to death.

THE CONFRONTATION

David followed Saul out of the cave and shouted after him: "My lord the king!" Saul turned around and saw David bowing face-down on the ground.

"Why do you listen to people who say I'm trying to harm you?" David called out. "Look what happened today! The LORD delivered you into my hands in the cave. Some urged me to kill you, but I spared you. I said, 'I will not lift my hand against my master, because he is the LORD's anointed.'"

Then David held up the piece of Saul's robe. "See, my father? Look at this piece of your robe in my hand! I cut off the corner of your robe but did not kill you. Doesn't this prove I'm not guilty of rebellion? I have not wronged you, but you are hunting me down to take my life."

David made his case powerfully. He could have killed Saul. He had every human reason to do so. But he chose to let God be the judge between them.

"May the LORD judge between you and me," David declared. "May the LORD avenge the wrongs you have done to me, but my hand will not touch you."

Saul listened, and something broke in him—at least for the moment. "Is that your voice, David my son?" he asked, and he wept aloud. "You are more righteous than I. You have treated me well, but I have treated you badly."

Then Saul made an astonishing admission: "I know that you will surely be king and that the kingdom of Israel will be established in your hands." Saul knew. He had known for a long time. That's why he was so desperate to kill David—not because David had done anything wrong, but because Saul was fighting against what God had already decided.

Saul asked David to swear that when he became king, he wouldn't wipe out Saul's family. David gave his oath. Then Saul went home, and David went back to hiding.

Because David didn't trust Saul's tears. He knew better.

THE FOOL AND HIS SHEEP

Between the two cave encounters comes a different kind of story—one that almost made David act exactly like the violent king he refused to become.

A wealthy man named Nabal lived in the area. His name

literally meant "fool," and he lived up to it. He owned three thousand sheep and a thousand goats. During shearing season—a time of celebration and feasting—David sent messengers to Nabal with a respectful request.

David's men had been protecting Nabal's shepherds and flocks in the wilderness. They hadn't taken anything; they hadn't harassed anyone. They had been like a wall of protection. Now David asked if Nabal might share some food from his abundance.

Nabal's response was insulting. "Who is this David? Who is this son of Jesse? Many servants are breaking away from their masters these days. Why should I take my bread and water and meat and give it to men coming from who knows where?"

The messengers returned and told David what Nabal had said. David's response was immediate and terrifying: "Put on your swords!"

Four hundred armed men marched toward Nabal's property. David was done being disrespected. He swore an oath: by morning, not one male in Nabal's household would be left alive. David was about to commit mass murder over an insult.

THE WOMAN WHO SAVED TWO MEN

One of Nabal's servants ran to Nabal's wife, Abigail. Unlike her foolish husband, Abigail was intelligent and beautiful. The servant explained the situation: David's men had protected them, Nabal had insulted David, and now disaster was coming.

Abigail didn't waste time arguing with her fool of a husband. She gathered supplies—bread, wine, sheep, grain, raisins, figs—loaded them on donkeys, and rode out to intercept David.

When she saw him, she got off her donkey and bowed face-down before him. "Please let me speak," she said. "Pay no attention to that wicked man Nabal. He is just like his name—his name means Fool, and folly goes with him."

Then Abigail delivered one of the wisest speeches in the entire Bible. She reminded David of who he was and who he was becoming. "The LORD will certainly make a lasting dynasty for my lord, because you fight the LORD's battles. Throughout your lifetime, no evil will be found in you. Even though someone is pursuing you to take your life, your life will be bound securely in the bundle of the living by the LORD your God."

Then came the key point: "When the LORD has done for my lord every good thing he promised and has appointed you ruler over Israel, don't let this be a staggering burden to you—that you shed innocent blood or avenged yourself. And when the LORD has brought you success, remember your servant."

Abigail was saying: Don't do this. You're going to be king. Don't stain your hands with unnecessary blood. Don't let anger make you do something you'll regret for the rest of your life.

David listened. His rage cooled. He saw what he had almost done. "Praise be to the LORD, the God of Israel, who has sent you today to meet me," David said. "May you be blessed for your good judgment and for keeping me from bloodshed this day and from avenging myself with my own hands." He accepted her gifts and sent her home in peace.

About ten days later, God struck Nabal dead. And David—recognizing both her wisdom and her character—sent for Abigail and made her his wife.

The lesson was clear: David didn't need to take vengeance. God would handle it. David's job was to keep his hands clean and trust God's timing.

THE SPEAR AND THE WATER JUG

The lesson came just in time. Because soon David faced his second test with Saul.

The Ziphites again betrayed David's location to Saul. Once more, Saul gathered three thousand soldiers and came hunting. This time David decided not to run.

He took Abishai, one of his toughest warriors, and they snuck into Saul's camp at night. They found Saul sleeping in the center of the camp, surrounded by his army, with his spear stuck in the ground by his head and his water jug beside him.

"Today God has delivered your enemy into your hands," Abishai whispered. "Let me pin him to the ground with one thrust of the spear. I won't need to strike him twice."

Here it was again. Another perfect opportunity. Another chance to end the running and hiding. God had clearly made this happen—everyone in the camp was in a deep sleep.

But David said no. "Don't destroy him! Who can lay a hand on the LORD's anointed and be guiltless? As surely as the LORD lives, the LORD himself will strike him, or his time will come and he will die, or he will go into battle and perish. But the LORD forbid that I should lay a hand on the LORD's anointed."

David was even more confident now than he had been in the cave. After watching God deal with Nabal, David knew for certain: God didn't need David's help to remove Saul. God would handle it in his own way and his own time. David's job was to stay faithful and wait.

Instead of killing Saul, David took his spear and water jug. Then he and Abishai slipped away without anyone waking up—because, the text tells us, "the LORD had put them into a deep sleep."

THE FINAL CONVERSATION

From a safe distance, David shouted across the valley, mocking Abner, Saul's general: "Aren't you a great man? Who is like you in Israel? Why didn't you guard your lord the king? Someone came to destroy him! You deserve to die! Look around—where are the king's spear and water jug that were near his head?"

Saul recognized David's voice. "Is that you, David my son?"

"Yes, my lord the king," David answered. "Why is my lord pursuing his servant? What have I done? What wrong am I guilty of?"

Then David poured out his heart. Saul's pursuit was driving him out of Israel—away from the land where God's people worshiped, away from the tabernacle and the sacrifices, away from everything that connected him to God's presence. David wasn't complaining about danger; he was grieving about being cut off from worship.

Saul confessed again: "I have sinned. Come back, David my son. I will not try to harm you again. Surely I have acted like a fool and have erred greatly."

But David didn't come back. He didn't trust Saul's promises—and he was right not to. Instead, he simply said, "Here is the king's spear. Let one of your men come and get it. The

LORD rewards everyone for their righteousness and faithfulness. He delivered you into my hands today, but I would not lay a hand on the LORD's anointed."

Saul blessed David and predicted his success. Then they parted ways.

They never saw each other again.

WHAT THIS MEANS FOR US

First, God's will must be achieved in God's way. David knew God had promised him the kingdom. But he refused to take it by killing God's anointed king. The right goal achieved through wrong means is still wrong. The end doesn't justify the means.

Second, restraint requires more strength than revenge. Anyone can lash out when they're hurt. It takes real power—and real faith—to hold back when you have every opportunity to strike. David's self-control in those caves required more courage than any battle.

Third, anger can make us do things we'll regret forever. David was about to massacre Nabal's household over an insult. He would have lived with that guilt for the rest of his life. Abigail saved him from himself. We need people who will speak truth to us when we're blinded by rage.

Fourth, God doesn't need our help to judge our enemies. David learned this with Nabal: God struck the fool dead within ten days. David didn't need to dirty his hands. Our job isn't to take revenge—it's to trust God's justice.

Fifth, sometimes faithfulness means waiting. David could have become king years earlier if he'd killed Saul. But he would have become a different kind of king—one who seized power through murder. By waiting, David proved he was the kind of king God wanted.

TALKING POINTS

1. **David felt guilty just for cutting Saul's robe.** Why do you think such a small symbolic act bothered his conscience so much?

2. **Abigail risked her life to stop David from doing something terrible.** What made her willing to take that risk? How can we be like Abigail for our friends?

3. **David said he wouldn't lay a hand on "the LORD's anointed."** What does this teach us about respecting people in positions of authority, even when they don't deserve it?

4. **The second time David spared Saul, he was more confident about waiting for God's timing.** How did the Nabal experience change him?

5. **Saul admitted twice that David would be king, yet he kept hunting him.** Why do you think people sometimes fight against what they know is true?

Two caves. Two chances to kill. Two decisions to trust God instead. David walked away from both encounters with clean hands. He would become king—not by murder, but by patience. Not by seizing, but by receiving.

The kingdom was worth waiting for. So was the kind of king he would become.

Turn the page.

9

LIVING WITH THE ENEMY

In *Captain America: Civil War*, Steve Rogers finds himself in an impossible situation. He's caught between loyalty to his country and loyalty to his friend Bucky. No matter which way he turns, someone is going to get hurt. Every choice leads to consequences he doesn't want. He ends up becoming a fugitive—a hero with no home, living in the shadows, making complicated decisions just to survive.

Sometimes life puts you in situations where there are no clean options. Where every path forward involves compromise or risk. Where you're just trying to make it through one more day.

David knew that feeling. After years of running from Saul—hiding in caves, fleeing from town to town, watching friends die because they helped him—David finally hit a wall. He was exhausted. He looked at his situation and made a calculation: either keep running until Saul eventually catches me, or do something drastic.

He chose drastic. He went to live with the Philistines. It was a decision born of desperation. It was complicated and morally messy. But it also shows us something important about how God works—even when we make choices from fear rather than faith, God doesn't abandon us. He keeps working, keeps protecting, keeps moving us toward his purposes.

DAVID'S DESPERATE DECISION

"One of these days I will be destroyed by the hand of Saul," David said to himself. "The best thing I can do is escape to the land of the Philistines. Then Saul will give up searching for me."

This is a significant moment. David had twice spared Saul's life when he could have killed him. He had received promises from Jonathan and Abigail that God would make him king. He had experienced God's protection over and over again—the last-minute escapes, the providential rescues, the narrow deliverances.

But now? Now David looked at his circumstances and saw only danger. He stopped trusting what God had promised and started trusting what his eyes could see. And what his eyes saw was this: Saul would never stop hunting him. Eventually, the odds would catch up. Eventually, he would be "swept away."

So David took his six hundred men, their wives and children, and went to Achish, the king of Gath.

Yes, *that* Gath—the Philistine city, Goliath's hometown. The last time David went there, he had to pretend to be insane to escape. But things were different now. David wasn't a lone fugitive; he was the leader of a small army. And Achish saw an opportunity: if Israel's greatest warrior was willing to defect, the Philistines could use him.

When Saul heard that David had fled to Philistine territory, he finally stopped searching. David's gamble had worked—at least in terms of survival.

But at what cost?

THE TOWN CALLED ZIKLAG

Living in Gath was awkward. David and his hundreds of followers were crowding the royal city, and Achish was constantly watching. David needed more independence. "If I have found favor in your eyes," David said to Achish, "let a place be given to me in one of the country towns. Why should your servant live in the royal city with you?"

Achish agreed and gave David the town of Ziklag—a border town in the south that had originally been assigned to Israel but had fallen under Philistine control. David and his people settled there, and for the first time in years, they had a place to call home.

David lived in Philistine territory for a year and four months. During this time, David faced a dilemma. He was supposed to be serving Achish—raiding and fighting on behalf of the Philistines. But he couldn't attack his own people. So he came up with a scheme.

David and his men would raid the Geshurites, Girzites, and Amalekites—desert tribes living south of Judah who were enemies of Israel. Then David would return to Achish with plunder and report that he had been raiding the territory of Judah and its allies.

Achish was delighted. He thought David had made himself so hated by his own people that he could never go back. "He has become so odious to his people," Achish said to himself, "that he will be my servant forever."

David was playing a dangerous double game. He was deceiving Achish while secretly helping Israel by attacking their mutual enemies. To make sure no one exposed his deception, David left no survivors from his raids who might report what he was really doing.

It was morally complicated. The text doesn't praise or condemn David for this—it simply reports what he did. Sometimes survival requires difficult choices.

TRAPPED

Then came the crisis David had been dreading. The Philistines gathered their armies for a massive assault on Israel. This wasn't just a border skirmish—this was the full force of the Philistine military preparing for war. And Achish expected David to join them.

"Understand," Achish told David, "that you and your men are to go out with me in the army."

David's heart must have stopped. He had worked so hard to avoid exactly this situation. He couldn't fight against his own people. But he also couldn't reveal his true loyalties without getting himself and all his men killed.

His answer was masterfully ambiguous: "Very well, you shall know what your servant can do." It sounded like confident boasting. Achish took it as a promise of loyalty and made David his personal bodyguard.

But inside, David must have been panicking. How was he going to get out of this?

PROVIDENTIAL RESCUE

The Philistine forces assembled at Aphek, preparing to march north against Israel. The five Philistine lords reviewed their troops—and when they saw David and his men marching with Achish's forces, they were furious. "What about these Hebrews?" they demanded.

Achish defended David: "Is this not David, the servant of Saul king of Israel? He has been with me for over a year, and from the day he left Saul until now, I have found no fault in him."

But the other Philistine commanders weren't convinced. "Send the man back! He must not go with us into battle, or he'll turn against us during the fighting. How better could he regain his master's favor than by taking the heads of our own men? Isn't this the David they sang about: 'Saul has slain his thousands, and David his tens of thousands'?"

They didn't trust David. And who could blame them? David had built his reputation by killing Philistines. Now they were supposed to believe he would fight alongside them?

Achish had to break the news to David: "You have been reliable, and I would be pleased to have you serve with me. But the other lords don't approve. Go back in peace."

David protested—probably more for show than anything else: "But what have I done? What fault have you found in me?"

Inside, though, David must have been flooded with relief. The Philistine lords had just solved his impossible dilemma. He wouldn't have to fight against Israel after all.

God had rescued David through his enemies. The very people David feared had unwittingly saved him from betraying his own nation.

DISASTER AT ZIKLAG

But David's troubles weren't over. When he and his men made the three-day journey back to Ziklag, they found devastation.

The Amalekites had raided the town while David was away. They had burned Ziklag to the ground and carried off everything—all the women and children, all the possessions, everything. David's two wives, Ahinoam and Abigail, were gone. "David and his men wept aloud until they had no strength left to weep."

This was the lowest point of David's life. He had lost everything. His home was ashes. His family had been taken. And now his own men—the warriors who had followed him through years of hardship—were so bitter and angry that they talked of stoning him.

Think about that. David's own men wanted to kill him. They blamed him for leaving their families unprotected. After everything they had endured together, their grief had turned to rage, and that rage was directed at David.

He was utterly alone.

STRENGTHENED IN GOD

Then comes one of the most important sentences in all of 1 Samuel: "But David strengthened himself in the LORD his God."

In his darkest hour, with everything stripped away, David turned back to God. He didn't have Jonathan to encourage him. He didn't have Samuel to guide him. He didn't even have loyal men standing with him. All he had was God.

And that was enough.

David called for Abiathar the priest and the ephod—the

tool for inquiring of God. For the first time in this entire section, David sought God's direction. "Shall I pursue this raiding party? Will I overtake them?"

God answered: "Pursue them. You will certainly overtake them and succeed in the rescue." That was all David needed. Armed with God's promise, he set out with his six hundred men to chase the Amalekites.

THE EGYPTIAN IN THE FIELD

Two hundred of David's men were too exhausted to continue past the Besor Ravine. David left them with the supplies and pressed on with four hundred.

In the wilderness, they found an Egyptian slave—half dead from hunger and thirst. He had been abandoned by his Amalekite master three days earlier when he fell ill. David's men revived him with food, water, and figs.

"Who do you belong to?" David asked. "Where do you come from?"

"I am an Egyptian, the slave of an Amalekite," the man said. "My master abandoned me when I became ill three days ago. We raided the territory south of the Kerethites, and the land belonging to Judah, and the territory south of Caleb. And we burned Ziklag."

David asked, "Can you lead me to this raiding party?"

The Egyptian agreed—on the condition that David swear not to kill him or return him to his master. David gave his word. This abandoned slave became the key to David's victory. A small act of kindness—giving food and water to a dying man—led directly to the recovery of everything that had been lost.

TOTAL VICTORY

The Egyptian led David to the Amalekite camp. They found the raiders sprawled across the countryside, eating, drinking, and celebrating their massive haul of plunder. They thought they were safe.

They were wrong.

David attacked at twilight and fought them until evening the next day. It was a complete rout. Only four hundred young men escaped on camels. Everyone else was killed.

The victory was total. David recovered everything the Amalekites had taken—not just from Ziklag but from all their raids. His wives were safe. All the women and children were rescued. Nothing was missing, "whether small or great, sons or daughters, plunder or anything they had taken."

The text emphasizes the completeness: "David recovered all." God had kept his promise. David had pursued. David had overtaken. David had succeeded in the rescue.

GRACE FOR EVERYONE

When David returned to the two hundred men who had stayed behind at the Besor Ravine, some of the warriors who had fought complained. "Because they did not go out with us, we will not share the plunder with them. Let each man take his wife and children and go."

But David refused. "No, my brothers. You must not do that with what the LORD has given us. He protected us and delivered into our hands the raiding party that came against us."

Then David established a principle that would guide Israel's armies for generations: "The share of the man who stayed with the supplies is to be the same as the share of the man who went into battle. All will share alike."

David recognized that the victory—and everything it produced—was a gift from God. It wasn't payment for services rendered. It was grace. And grace is shared.

BUILDING FOR THE FUTURE

David did something else shrewd and generous. He sent portions of the plunder to the elders of various towns in Judah—places where he and his men had stayed during their years of running from Saul. "Here is a gift for you from the plunder of the LORD's enemies," he said.

It was partly gratitude—thanking communities that had helped him. It was partly compensation—some of these towns had likely suffered from Amalekite raids themselves. And it was partly political wisdom—building relationships with leaders who would soon be asked to accept him as their king.

David was no longer just surviving. He was preparing for what God had promised. The kingdom was coming, and David was getting ready.

WHAT THIS MEANS FOR US

First, even people of great faith have moments of fear. David's decision to flee to Philistia came from exhaustion and despair, not from trust in God. The Bible doesn't hide this. Faith isn't the absence of fear—it's returning to God despite our fears.

Second, God works even through our compromised situations. David's time with the Philistines was morally complicated. But God still protected him, still guided him, still used that season to prepare him for kingship. Our mistakes don't cancel God's purposes.

Third, small kindnesses can have huge consequences. David gave food to a dying Egyptian slave. That simple act led to the recovery of everything he had lost. Never underestimate the power of compassion.

Fourth, when everything is stripped away, God remains. David strengthened himself in the Lord his God when he had absolutely nothing else. That's the foundation that holds when everything else collapses.

Fifth, grace is meant to be shared. David insisted that everyone share equally in the plunder—those who fought and those who guarded the supplies. What God gives us isn't earned, so we shouldn't hoard it.

TALKING POINTS

1. **David decided to flee to Philistia because he thought he would eventually be "destroyed by Saul."** What does this show us about how even strong believers can struggle with fear?

2. **The Philistine lords refused to let David fight against Israel—which solved David's impossible dilemma.** How do you see God's providence working through people who didn't even know they were helping?

3. **When David's men wanted to stone him, "he strengthened himself in the LORD his God."** What do you think that looked like practically? How can we do the same thing when we're at our lowest?

4. **David showed kindness to the abandoned Egyptian slave, and that kindness led to his victory.** Can you think

of a time when a small act of kindness led to something much bigger?

5. David insisted that those who guarded the supplies should share equally with those who fought. Why was this principle so important? How does it connect to grace?

David had gone to Philistia running from Saul. He came back running toward his destiny.

The journey had been messy—full of deception, moral compromise, and near-disasters. But through it all, God had been working. Protecting. Guiding. Preparing.

Sometimes the path to God's purposes leads through enemy territory. But even there, he never lets go.

Turn the page.

10

THE FALL OF THE KING

In *Star Wars: Revenge of the Sith*, we watch Anakin Skywalker's final transformation into Darth Vader. It's heartbreaking because we remember who he used to be—the hopeful young Jedi, the hero of countless battles, the one who was supposed to bring balance to the Force. But fear led to anger, anger led to hate, and hate led to his destruction. By the end of the movie, the man we once cheered for has become unrecognizable.

Saul's story ends the same way. This was the tall, handsome young man who hid among the baggage because he didn't want to be king. The one the Spirit of God rushed upon. The one who rescued Jabesh-gilead and united the tribes. Samuel had called him the one "on whom is all the desire of Israel."

Now, in his final hours, we find Saul disguised in ordinary clothes, sneaking through enemy lines at night to visit a witch. The contrast is devastating.

This is how a king falls—not all at once, but one choice at a time, until the person who remains bears little resemblance to the person who started.

TERROR IN THE NIGHT

The Philistines had gathered their full military force for a massive invasion. This wasn't a border raid—this was an army intent on crushing Israel once and for all. They camped at Shunem, in the Valley of Jezreel, positioning themselves to cut Israel in half and control the major trade routes.

Saul gathered his army at Mount Gilboa, a few miles to the south. When he looked across the valley and saw the size of the Philistine forces, "he was afraid; terror filled his heart."

In the past, Saul would have inquired of God. So he tried. He sought answers through dreams—nothing. Through the Urim (the priestly way of seeking God's guidance)—nothing. Through prophets—nothing.

God was silent.

This was the consequence Saul had been warned about. When you persistently refuse to listen to God's voice, eventually God stops speaking. When you repeatedly reject God's word, eventually God's word is taken from you.

Saul had dismissed Samuel. He had slaughtered the priests at Nob. He had spent years chasing David instead of leading Israel. Now, facing the crisis of his life, he discovered that the God he had ignored for so long would not answer him.

The silence must have been terrifying.

THE WITCH OF ENDOR

In his desperation, Saul made a decision that revealed how far he had fallen. "Find me a woman who is a medium," he told his servants, "so I may go and inquire of her."

A medium was someone who claimed to communicate

with the dead. God's law strictly forbade this practice—it was one of the reasons God had driven out the nations who lived in Canaan before Israel. Saul himself had enforced this law, expelling mediums and spiritists from the land. Now he was seeking one out.

His servants knew exactly where to find such a woman—in a town called Endor. Saul disguised himself, put on ordinary clothes, and traveled there at night with two men. They had to slip past Philistine lines to reach her, adding danger to desperation.

When they arrived, the woman was suspicious. "You know what Saul has done," she said. "He has cut off the mediums from the land. Why are you setting a trap for me?"

Saul swore an oath—by the Lord, no less—that she would not be punished. The irony is thick: Saul invoked God's name to guarantee safety for breaking God's law.

"Whom shall I bring up for you?" she asked.

"Bring up Samuel."

A MESSAGE FROM BEYOND

What happened next has puzzled readers for centuries. When the woman performed her ritual, she screamed. She saw Samuel—and she also suddenly realized her client was Saul.

"Why have you deceived me? You are Saul!"

The king reassured her and asked what she saw. "An old man wearing a robe is coming up," she said.

Saul knew it was Samuel. He bowed face-down to the ground.

Samuel was not happy to be disturbed. "Why have you brought me up?" he demanded.

"I am in great distress," Saul said. "The Philistines are fighting against me, and God has turned away from me. He no longer answers me, either by prophets or by dreams. So I have called on you to tell me what to do."

Samuel's response was blunt and brutal: "Why do you consult me, now that the LORD has turned away from you and become your enemy? The LORD has done what he predicted through me. The LORD has torn the kingdom out of your hands and given it to David."

Then came the prophecy Saul dreaded most: "The LORD will hand over both Israel and you to the Philistines, and tomorrow you and your sons will be with me."

Tomorrow. Saul and his sons would be dead by tomorrow.

Saul collapsed. He fell full length on the ground, paralyzed with fear, weakened by having eaten nothing all day. The woman and his servants eventually convinced him to eat something before the long journey back to his army.

He ate his last meal in a medium's house, preparing to face a battle he knew he would lose.

THE BATTLE OF MOUNT GILBOA

The next day, the Philistines attacked. It was a slaughter. The Israelites fled before them, and many fell dead on Mount Gilboa. The Philistines pressed hard after Saul and his sons, determined to wipe out the royal family.

They killed Jonathan.

Stop and feel the weight of that. Jonathan—the faithful friend, the brave warrior, the man who loved David and accepted that David would be king instead of him. Jonathan, who had said, "Go in peace, for we have sworn friendship with each other in the name of the LORD." Jonathan, who deserved so much better than to die on this bloody hillside because of his father's failures.

They also killed Abinadab and Malki-Shua, Saul's other sons.

The fighting grew fierce around Saul himself. Philistine archers found their mark, and Saul was critically wounded.

He knew it was over. And he knew what the Philistines would do to him if they captured him alive—they would torture him and humiliate him. He turned to his armor-bearer. "Draw your sword and run me through," Saul said, "or these uncircumcised fellows will come and abuse me."

But the armor-bearer was terrified and refused. He couldn't bring himself to strike the LORD's anointed, even at the king's own request.

So Saul took his own sword and fell on it. When the armor-bearer saw that Saul was dead, he did the same. Saul, his three sons, and his armor-bearer all died together that day.

THE AFTERMATH

When Israelites living in the surrounding region heard that the army had fled and that Saul and his sons were dead, they abandoned their towns. The Philistines moved in and occupied them. It was a catastrophic defeat—Israel had lost its king, its princes, and significant territory in a single day.

The next morning, the Philistines returned to the battlefield to strip the dead. They found the bodies of Saul and his sons on Mount Gilboa.

They cut off Saul's head. They stripped off his armor. They sent messengers throughout Philistia to proclaim the victory in the temples of their idols. They put Saul's armor in the temple of their goddess Ashtoreth.

Then they fastened the bodies of Saul and his sons to the wall of Beth-shan—a public display of triumph and humiliation.

It seemed like the ultimate defeat. The Philistine gods had won. Israel's God had been proven powerless to protect his king.

ONE FINAL ACT OF LOYALTY

But the story doesn't quite end there. The people of Jabesh-gilead heard what the Philistines had done to Saul's body. They remembered. Decades earlier, when the Ammonites had threatened to gouge out the right eye of every man in their city, Saul had marched through the night to rescue them. He had been their deliverer.

Now it was their turn.

All the valiant men of Jabesh-gilead set out on a dangerous nighttime mission. They traveled through Philistine-controlled territory to Beth-shan—about a twenty-mile round trip. They took down the bodies of Saul and his sons from the wall. They brought them back to Jabesh and gave them proper burial. Then they fasted for seven days.

It was a small act of dignity in the midst of disaster. It couldn't undo the defeat. It couldn't bring back the dead. But it said something important: we remember. We are grateful. Even in death, we will honor the man who once saved us.

Saul's reign began with rescuing Jabesh-gilead. It ended with Jabesh-gilead rescuing him.

WHAT THIS MEANS FOR US

First, small compromises lead to great disasters. Saul didn't become the man in the medium's house overnight. He got there one disobedient choice at a time—keeping Agag alive, offering the sacrifice himself, prioritizing his reputation over God's commands. Sin is progressive. The ending is written in the beginning.

Second, God's silence is the consequence of persistent rejection. Saul wanted God's guidance when he was terrified, but he had spent years ignoring God's word when it was inconvenient. God is patient, but he will not be mocked. Those who repeatedly reject his voice may find that voice withdrawn.

Third, our choices affect those we love. Jonathan died on Gilboa. He died because of a battle his father couldn't win, in a war his father had neglected while chasing David. The innocent often suffer because of the sins of others.

Fourth, even failed lives can be treated with dignity. The men of Jabesh-gilead didn't pretend Saul was perfect. But they honored him anyway, remembering the good he had done. There is grace even in grief.

Fifth, this is not the end of the story. First Samuel closes in darkness—a dead king, a defeated nation, bodies hanging on a wall. But the reader knows that David is waiting. A new king is coming. Morning will follow this terrible night.

TALKING POINTS

1. **Saul sought God's guidance only when he was desperate, after ignoring God for years.** Why do you think God

didn't answer him? What does this teach us about our relationship with God?

2. **Jonathan died alongside his father even though he had been faithful to both God and David.** How do you make sense of the innocent suffering because of others' sins?

3. **The men of Jabesh-gilead risked their lives to honor Saul's body.** Why was this important? What does gratitude require of us?

4. **Saul's story is one of wasted potential—he had every advantage and threw it all away.** What warning does his life offer us?

5. **First Samuel ends in tragedy, but the story continues in 2 Samuel with David becoming king.** How does knowing "the rest of the story" change how we read difficult endings?

The king who once stood head and shoulders above everyone else now lay fallen on Mount Gilboa.

But somewhere to the south, David was still alive. God's promise still stood. The shepherd-king was coming.

Even in the darkest night, dawn was on its way.

www.ingramcontent.com/pod-product-compliance
Lightning Source LLC
Chambersburg PA
CBHW051413050726
47595CB00010B/4051